BUILT FOR **ETERNITY**

TOOLS FOR BUILDING A SOLID SPIRITUAL FOUNDATION FOR OUR CHILDREN

Patience Irete

Praises for Built for Eternity

Today, many forces are contesting for our children's attention as they grow up. Never before has raising godly children, in all that pertains to life and godliness, been a more Herculean task than today. In this book, **Built for Eternity**, Sister Patience Irete draws from her wealth of experience garnered from years of involvement with children, as a parent, and as a minister in the Children Ministry. She gives us a wide variety of nuggets that not only bear directly on her practical experience but also irradiates her thoughts on issues of fundamental importance and relevance. This book is rich and instructive. It focuses not only on Christian parenting but also on the need for parents to live a Christ-like life that is apparent to their children and others to emulate.

In conclusion, I would like to echo the voice of the author in the *Preface* to the book: "So, thank you for the decision to pick up this book to read. I can, with all humility, tell you that it is not just another book, but a call to action for parents and carers." Remain abundantly blessed.

*** Rev. Dr. Dapo Adeleke, Sydney, Australia***

Built for Eternity is a masterpiece born out of passion, not only for helping families raise Godly children but to help attain the ultimate goal of making eternity. As a close observer of the writer, Sister Pat has consistently demonstrated her love for children and family fulfillment. This book is a summary of a life dedicated to this all-important call. I encourage you not only to read but follow each recommended step in this book. Thank you, Sister Pat, for letting this piece out of your inner being for the world to be blessed thereby. We are indeed waiting for the next episode!

*** Pastor Gabriel Oyeniran, Canada***

I highly recommend **Built for Eternity** to all parents, guardians, and mentors who desire to instill Godly principles in their children. It is not just a book but a practical guide that provides the tools required to raise a generation of children who are passionate about living for Christ. The reflective questions and exercises at the end of each chapter make it even more engaging and appealing to the reader. Thank you, Aunt Pat, for blessing us with this resourceful masterpiece.

Wanemi Uko (Eke-Spiff), Canada

This book has been in my mom's heart for a long time, and it has been a point of pride for the whole family to watch her nurture this project and bring it to this point. The book shares the tools and principles she has picked up not just from raising us but in working with youth and families professionally as well. I know there will be something useful in it for everyone.

Oseremen Dan Irete, Canada

I am incredibly proud of my mom for finishing this book. When she first mentioned it, I was not sure how she would combine writing a book while working full time, volunteering in the church, and raising a family. It was motivating for me to see her finish this book as well as just seeing her work on it from start to finish. My mom has always been involved with children, which I think equipped her to write this book. I am excited to see how this book will impact the lives of the readers.

Isibhakhomen Esther Irete, Canada

I am very proud of my mom for finishing her first book, notwithstanding all the other commitments and priorities she faces daily. **Built for Eternity** is an expression of the commitment she has for children, raising four children, and mentoring many others.

Efeose Anita Deborah Irete

Patience Egbathioh Irete (aka My D) is my friend, heartthrob, and soul mate of over 25 years. As a family, we join her to offer matchless gratitude to God Almighty for salvation, numerous testimonies, and the journey of her life thus far!

We are humbled and grateful for the vital message of hope, encouragement, and inspiration to homes, parents, caregivers, and children. Our God indeed is a God, with whom; nothing shall be impossible (Luke 1v37).

Typically, we are a family that is knitted together and very much into books, academics, school, and the likes. However, if anyone were to hazard a guess on which of us would write or publish a book first, I believe none would have picked her.

Over the years, I have witnessed her battles, victories, tests, testimonies, strength, and the tenacity to excel. Nothing she does surprises me anymore. She has always been an enigma of a sort, one who defies odds and people's expectations.

Therefore, when with an unusual shuddering voice, she broke the news that God had laid in her heart to write books (books – not a book); I had a little laugh with a smirk on my face! Not because she was not capable - far from it, but because it took me by surprise, given all she had on her plate to contend with at the time. She seriously struggled with it, but it will not go away! As if to prove beyond any doubt that it was of God, there were not just revelations and confirmations from far and near; God immediately began to arrange, connect and bring resourceful individuals and destiny helpers that took away her doubts and fears gradually.

I testify with all in me that My D loves God and people and has all her life been passionate about children and their total well-being and bringing them up in the way of the Lord. A virtuous woman in every sense of the word who is a strong believer in inculcating and living strong Christian family values. She, as a young educated wife and mother, sacrificed her personal ambition and prospect of a glamorous professional career and opted rather take on only ventures and opportunities that would make her available as much as possible for her children and family. Little wonder that in her secular life, she is a trained social worker who works with children and families. As a worker in the church, she is a committed and dedicated children's teacher for many years. She is 'Sister Pat' to her theming children admirers.

I, therefore, have no doubt that the book *Built for Eternity,* which you have in your hands or device, is not just another book! It is God's inspired message to every parent, caregiver, family, and child through a lovely soul for the benefit and greater good of our world. Read it, use it, treasure it, and see God impact and prepare a solid foundation in this world and unto eternity for every child under your care and influence, by His grace and mercy!

Alex Irete, Canada

BUILT FOR **ETERNITY**

TOOLS FOR BUILDING A SOLID SPIRITUAL FOUNDATION FOR OUR CHILDREN

Patience Irete

This book is dedicated to all the parents and caregivers who set out to invest their resources, and will not give up on the children, because we want the best in life for them, and want them to inherit eternal life.

Contents

Foreword

Raising five children is not a job for the faint-hearted. It is a job that requires ample patient, perseverance, and grace! Grace! Grace! That is probably why five in the Bible represent GRACE!

Parenting is a job that nobody can ever adequately prepare for. There is no school, no try before you buy or return if damaged or unwanted, that can adequately prepare you for what lies ahead. It is a role that you learn on the job and are expected to be perfect immediately. There is pressure to be excellent communicators, mind readers, and jugglers of activities and your children's educators. Each mistake is magnified and comes with guilt and self-condemnation before society wakes up to condemn you.

I have learned over the last twenty-five years of raising my family that each child is unique and comes with their own goodness and challenges. Thanks to the help of resources and encouragement that is in line with my faith, I have learned to train and raise my family in the way they should go, doing my best and leaving the rest to God. *But it did not come easy!*

Built for Eternity is an excellent resource for every parent to help in the quest for information, inspiration, and education, both physically and spiritually. Patience Irete has done a great job of simplifying some of the tools and shows us that we are not alone. She shares her passion for children, to start early in their lives, and to focus on building strong relationships instead of a dictatorship role. She recognizes the importance of investing time, and investing in their

1

talents, supporting their decisions, having faith in God, and committing their future into His hands.

As you read this book, I pray that it will open your eyes to understand that parenting is a gift from God, and each child is a gift, and to be grateful to God for them.

Be blessed as you read
Pastor Dee Adekugbe
All Woman Ministry

The Birth of the Vision

When the Lord spoke to my heart to write a book, I smiled and thought to myself, "Me, write a book!? Me? My essays were always saddled with run-on sentences!" But God had spoken and not man. I mentioned it to my husband after about three weeks, and the answer was…yes! There were three full weeks of inner struggle and head dialogue, and of course, he laughed too.

This was at a time in my life when things were not as easy as they appeared. Neither my family, finances, nor my health was in good shape. I was not mentally, spiritually, or emotionally at my best. Before now, I was putting resources together to set up a program, one that would have people come together to talk about building a solid spiritual foundation for our children. I wanted a program; God wanted a book!

In my quest to learn how and what would be needed, I made some connections in town, including looking online. It was during one of those days that I stumbled on a Facebook advert about Deborah's Company put together by the ever-cheerful Pastor Dee Adekugbe. Pastor Dee is the co-pastor of the Calgary-based World Harvest Christian Centre. I heard the Lord clearly saying I must meet her. I registered and attended the program, which was a life-transforming event for me. The Lord ministered to me expressly, and I wept almost all through the service. When it was ministration time, I wanted Pastor Dee to pray with me, but God had other plans for me. I was on the line to be ministered to by her, but she kept passing me.

I heard the Holy Spirit whisper gently, "Let me do my job. Relax." I relaxed, closed my eyes, and submitting myself to His plans for me that night. I was ushered gently to the lineup of those waiting to

3

be prayed for by our amiable Pastor Evelyn Brisibe of The Redeemed Christian Church of God (RCCG) Cornerstone Chapel. At this point, I was sobbing profusely, as the power of God moved mightily. She held my hands gently and whispered softly into my ears: "The Lord said, 'you should let go and let Him.'" I sobbed more! I prayed for the grace to let go. Still, I did not put pen to paper. I was still making human calculations, thinking about how I would go about it, rather than merely submitting to His will.

On August 6th, 2018, I was feeling emotional with my health and finances. My family was shocked when I told them I was not going to the Wednesday service without a tangible reason. I felt I just needed some quiet time alone. After they left, I logged on to Facebook and saw that "Joy Overflow" church was live, and I decided to watch. The message was prophetic, soul-lifting, and imparting. A word came through Pastor Sunny Adeniyi—the presiding pastor of Joy Overflow International Church, Calgary, Canada, about getting up and doing what God has called you to do. He said, "if it's to write a book, write it!" That was all I needed. At the end of the broadcast, I got up, got on my computer, and wrote the cover page to this book.

God used three ministry giants to birth this vision and to let the world know that indeed *Built for Eternity* is His heart's desire for us. It is a desire to build a solid spiritual foundation for His gifts to us—our children. I am indeed honored. You are not just holding a book; you are exploring the mind of God for mankind!

God Bless You!

Preface

Writing a book is not something I would have regarded as an achievement in my lifetime. I am the kind of person who has seen writing potential in everyone around me, but not in me. I have always had the privilege of working with children. During my little sojourn in The Netherlands, I was serving in the children's church nursery. During my secular job in Nigeria, I had an event planning outfit (event and resources). The part I enjoyed most was overseeing children's birthday parties. I remembered growing up in my place of birth, Oshodi, a boisterous suburb in Lagos, Nigeria, and our house was a meeting place for neighborhood children. I remember vividly on my eighteenth birthday that more than half of my guests were children. Almost every child on the street was in my home. For my impressionable fellow teens and young adult friends, this was not funny. I wish I still had photos from that day to show. There was little I could offer these children than my smile and some little teachings on morals, as I did not have much of a spiritual foundation myself.

Talking about the spiritual foundation. My parents, as far as I can remember, did not prevent my siblings or me from going to church when we chose to, though they were passive about religion and faith. Given such a scenario in a home, what child would wake up on a Sunday morning to get dressed and go to church by him/herself? That child was certainly not me! However, as fate would have it, a neighbor that all the children fondly called aunty Fausat took an interest in my spiritual life. She was born into a Muslim family and faith but converted to Christianity, subsequently changing her name to Bola. Looking back, I can boldly say she was fervent for the Lord. She was a member of her church choir, which meant to go to church, I had to wake up early to set out with her. We attended the Christ Apostolic Church, Powerline Agege, Lagos, in the Western part of Nigeria.

The changes in my life caused my parents to appreciate me going to church. Still, they were less enthusiastic about the extent of time we spent away from home. Most Sundays, we would leave home at about 8 a.m. and not return until about 4 p.m.! I returned home, looking, and feeling exhausted. Naturally, it was not long before my parents' concerns stopped me from going to church anymore. Soon after, aunty Bola got married and moved away from our neighborhood.

I am eternally grateful to God for using aunty Bola to sow the seed of the Christian faith. The hunger for God and church had been stirred up in me forever. Too late to go back now, I would say! Afterward, I tried to attend church with as many of my neighbors as time and opportunity permitted. Still, none of them were like "aunty Bola's church." Thank you, aunty Bola, for introducing Jesus Christ to the neighborhood children and me. As you can see, your labor of love was not in vain.

While in college, I joined the school fellowship. I had given my life to Christ by then, but I was one of those that we called "Campus Christians." I did not have a home church, which was a big struggle for me because consciously or unconsciously, I was looking for a church like aunty Bola's church. I, however, ended up going to The Deeper Life Bible Church whenever I was home on school breaks. Shortly after my marriage, I joined my husband in The New Generation Bible Church under Bishop G. I. Elomobor.

As I mentioned earlier, I am drawn to helping and working with children. I have always been surrounded by them. As I began to make myself available to God, He began to use me to invest in their spiritual lives. Seun and Sayo Yussuf, with some of their cousins, were part of the children I mentored. Taking after aunty Bola, you would say! Seun was about seven years old when we started going to church together.

She had health challenges at the time, which only drew us closer. Many times we prayed together and experienced the acts of the miracle-working God. Anytime she had a crisis, we prayed together; I would anoint her and command peace to come upon her. Today, my baby is doing very well, and to the glory of the Lord, she is in the music ministry. She is a testimony! She is my testimony! Seun was born with sickle cell anemia (SCA), but the Lord has kept her and will uphold her to the very end. She is married, and the union is blessed with a child! Only God could have done this. Praise be to God!

So, thank you for the decision to pick up this book to read. I can, with all humility, tell you that it is not just another book. This book is a call to action for parents and caregivers to begin to pay closer attention to the spiritual foundation of their children. Yes, we want them to excel and succeed in life. We invest time and resources and pay close attention to their academic, extracurricular activities, emotional needs, and success. But we inadvertently leave their spiritual upbringing to chance and Sunday school teachers, where they spend a few hours every Sunday. There is an urgent need for a paradigm shift. That is why when the Lord laid it in my heart to put this book together, I was not sure I was hearing the Lord correctly. Nonetheless, my confidence is that our God is a God of grace, who qualifies the called and enables us to will and to do His good pleasure.

In 1 Corinthians 1:27 (KJV), the Bible says, *"But God hath chosen the foolish things of the world to confound the wise, and God hath chosen the weak things of the world to confound the things which are mighty."* That same God who makes a way where there seems to be no way would miraculously bring people in my path who have walked hand in hand with me on this journey, all with the aim, I believe, to make this book a reality. I am eternally humbled and grateful.

To Him alone be all the Praise!

Introduction

The foundation of a structure can be regarded as the most crucial part of it, be it a physical structure, a dream, a vision, actualizing a goal, or starting a venture. It is the part that is often hidden, yet the whole essence of the structure is dependent on it. What a structure can hold later is dependent on the work, materials, and efforts that have gone into its foundation. Laying the right foundation to reach an important goal or aspiration is not a quick fix, as told to us in 2 Chronicles 31:7. *"In the third month, they began to lay the foundation of the heaps and finished them in the* seventh *month"* (KJV). Foundations—ethical foundations––are to be laid carefully, deliberately, and purposefully.

Referencing 2 Chronicles 31:7, note that the foundation was started in the third month and finished in the seventh month. There was no record that the job was ever stopped at any point in time during that period. It took four months of continuous, concentrated effort to build and lay the foundation. We must bear in mind the purpose for which it was being laid so the overall structure would not be compromised in any way.

This book aims to bring to our consciousness the importance of building a solid spiritual foundation for our children. As they journey through life, the inevitable winds of life would rage. The right foundation is a must for our children so that they are, by God's grace, able to stand and overcome, similar to a house that is built on solid ground. When the inevitable wind of trials and hardship came, the house still stood! *"And the rain fell, and the flood came, and the winds blew and beat on that house, but it did not fall, because it has been founded on the rock"* (Mathew 7:25 ESV).

It is essential to mention that the intent of this book is not to put anyone's parenting skills and abilities under scrutiny. Our goal is to create the needed awareness for all of us as parents to explore available help and tools for building a solid spiritual foundation for our children. Psalms 11:3 sums it up thusly: *"If the foundations be destroyed, what can the righteous do"* (KJV). The Lord strengthen our hands to build in whatever capacity He has placed us, in Jesus' mighty name. Amen!!!

The Foundation

In Psalm 104:5, the word of God declares, *"He set the earth on its foundations; it can never be moved."* (NIV). This Scripture testifies that the foundation of the earth was laid by God, the Father.

First Corinthians 3:11 (NLT) states, *"For no one can lay any foundation other than the one we already have—Jesus Christ."* This makes us understand that even the foundation of our faith was laid by our Lord and Savior, Jesus Christ.

In whatever we do in life, groundwork is needed. Within the context of this book, the spiritual foundation of our children is essential. This is so that when they are no longer under our direct supervision, they can stand. Just like Queen Esther, who was faced with the option of either enjoying the protection of her position or putting herself at personal risk, to save her people. She opted for the latter and declared, *"If I perish, I perish."*

In Esther 4:16 (KJV), Queen Esther stated; *"Go, gather together all the Jews that are present in Shushan, and fast ye for me, and neither eat nor drink three days, night or day: I also and my maidens will fast likewise; and so will I go in unto the king, which is not according to the law: and if I perish, I perish."*

Joseph is another example; he opted to remain faithful to godly ways rather than partake in an adulterous act with his master's wife. He declared, *"There is none greater in this house than I; neither hath he kept back anything from me but thee because thou art his wife: how then can I do this great wickedness and sin against God?"* (Genesis 39:9 KJV).

11

And like Shadrach, Meshach, and Abednego, who collectively refused to bow to a strange god despite the threats of death! They stood their grounds by declaring to the king with all boldness that *"But if not, be it known unto thee, O king, that we will not serve thy gods, nor worship the golden image which thou hast set up."* (Daniel 3:18 KJV).

Some might ask: When do I start building the spiritual foundation of my children and or the young lives under my care and influence? Permit me to ask: When do you start building the foundation of a house? Of course, it is the very moment you decide to build. When you choose to build, that is when you need to have a mental picture of all that is required, i.e., materials, people, artists, and much more. Above all, you start having a mental picture of the end product, even before the first brick is laid. The moment you decide to have children, you start speaking into their destinies.

Note that in the language of this book, as it goes on, I will be saying *we* and *us* instead of *you* and *your*. I am a mother, a woman, and a co-builder. I would also like to add that building a solid spiritual foundation for our children has nothing to do with gender or the roles that culture and society may have directly or indirectly assigned. It is the responsibility of every caring and responsible adult and caregiver, male or female, in the life of the child, in whatever capacity. As you read this book, whatever role you are positioned in or destined to play in the life of a child, do it as a committed builder.

Why Emphasize the Importance of Foundations?

"And the rain fell, and the floods came, and the winds blew and slammed against that house; and yet it did not fall, for it had been founded upon the rock. Everyone who hears these words of Mine and does not act on them will be like a foolish man who built his house on the sand. The rain fell, and the floods came, and the winds blew and slammed against that house, and it fell—and great was its fall." (Matthew 7:24-27 NASB).

In the above Scripture, Jesus gave a parable where He likened anyone that hears His word, keeps and does it, to one who builds his house on a rock, with a solid foundation.

As mentioned earlier, the floods of life will flow, winds of life will blow, and the rains of life will certainty fall. How have we prepared our children for these challenges? How we have developed our children or not for life's challenging times will always make and most likely be the difference. We will note in our Bible text that the house (a child, in this context) did not fall because the foundation was built upon the solid rock. The songwriter declares, "On Christ the solid Rock I stand, all other ground is sinking sand … All other ground is sinking sand." *All other ground* can be the situation the unprepared child finds himself or herself in. It is also important to note that the situation need not be unpleasant. Our children also need to be ready for how to handle successes. The wind, rain, or flood might be added responsibility associated with progress as they move up the ladder in life. Below are highlights of these elements.

Rain: According to Webster's dictionary, rain is "water condensed from atmospheric vapor and falling down upon the earth." This is necessary because of all the things it symbolizes. What then happens when that which the Lord has blessed us with now becomes a thorn in our flesh? Think about this for a moment. Now think of those overwhelming situations our children might have to go through at different stages of their lives. The essence of this book is to challenge our thought processes and start to have a "spiritual safety plan" for them. Rain symbolizes freshness, renewal, or rebirth. Anywhere rain is mentioned in the Bible, it signifies the presence of God. According to the Bible in Job 5:10 (KJV), it is God, "*Who giveth rain upon the earth, and sendeth waters upon the field:*" So, why is it that? What the Lord has created to nurture us has become an instrument of torture.

Flood: Flood, as defined by Webster dictionary, "is the overflowing of large amounts of water beyond its normal confines, breaking boundaries and barriers." Flooding can be likened to a continuous downpouring of rain when faced with situations, and it looks like there is no hope in sight. The rising of the sun each day gives birth to new challenges arriving in overwhelming quantities. That "house" can only stand if built upon the solid rock. Floods are mostly accompanied by powerful winds, leaving its victim in a devastating state after its visit. By the same token, the floods of life are no respecter of age, gender, race, or position. The *floods* of life in our children's lives can be as simple as wanting to belong, be accepted, or be respected. It could be adapting to a new environment, struggling with grades, or going to school without being bullied. It could also be meeting societal or family expectations, struggling with emotions and healthily facing emotions, etc.

Wind: Wind is "air in motion strong enough to be felt, with destructive or devastating effects" (Webster dictionary). Floods and rains are visible, but the wind is not! What skills, abilities, and words of life have been pumped into the life of the child, that when the wind of life blows, the child can stand after it passes away?

The Lord's Heritage

According to a dictionary definition, heritage is "something that comes or belongs to one because of birth; an inherited lot or portion." By this definition and with the Bible in the book of Psalm 127:3 corroborating, "Children are a gift from the Lord; they are a reward from him." (NLT).

We can deduce that the children God has blessed us with are His. Note the word "from" in that verse, for it has pleased Him to give them to us as "gifts." When we explore the mystery of gifts, it is the giver who decides what is befitting to give out at any particular time or event. The receiver of the gift has little or no say regarding the gift. Of course, there are situations where "requests" are made by the one expecting the gift. But typically, the giver calls the shots depending on the giver's capacity and/or circumstance. It is the same with the children God has given us to care for and nurture. It is our responsibility to care for them, being mindful that we will be held accountable by the giver of them. We are God's custodians, to nurture and build. That is why we

14

must be intentional and spare nothing as we invest our time, efforts, and resources to create and lay a solid spiritual foundation for them.

Gifts are treasures that come to us in various packages. There is a need to appreciate the giver. The easiest way to do so is to take care of the gift and maximize its potential. There have been cases where givers of gifts became displeased because they did not see the recipient put the gift to its intended use. Think about that for a moment: you gave someone a winter jacket as a birthday gift. There could be a couple of scenarios for this gift. Scenario 1: On the first day of winter, you notice someone elegantly decked in a lovely, hooded, feather-trimmed winter jacket. After a closer look, you realize it was the gift you gave them earlier in the year. Scenario 2: You never see this person wear the jacket (of course, they might have worn it), but you notice the coat in the trunk of their car amongst dirt and debris. How will you feel in either scenario?

Within the context of this book, children are gifts from God, and bringing them up in the way of the Lord should be our utmost priority. King Solomon wrote in the book of Proverbs that we should *"Train up a child in the way he should go: and when he is old, he will not depart from it."* (Proverbs 22:6 KJV).

I could not agree more that "training up a child" does not just involve the child to develop good habits, but also that the child can make appropriate decisions, and follow God, so they continue to do so well into adulthood[1] (Meredith Olson). She also highlighted two preconditions: the first is training—diligently teaching, correcting, and patiently explaining the reason behind your instruction. Hence, they fully understand and can apply it. Second is direction—the way is also translated as "road or path."

Consequently, the phrase "in the way he should go" refers to putting him on the right path. If you provide both training and the right direction, the end state is that the child will have that guidance for the rest of their life and apply it to stay on that path. When the child has grown, and the wind, the fire, or the floods of life begin to rage, the child can stand and declare like Job in Job 19:25a, *"For I know my redeemer liveth."*

15

Samuel was a gift to Hannah (she asked the Lord for a son), and Hannah embraced this gift. She nurtured this gift. Hannah returned Samuel to the temple in fulfillment of her vow to the Lord. *"And she vowed a vow, and said, O Lord of hosts, if thou wilt indeed look on the affliction of thine handmaid, and remember me, and not forget thine handmaid, but wilt give unto thine handmaid a man child, then I will give him unto the Lord all the days of his life, and there shall no razor come upon his head."* (1 Samuel 1:11 KJV).

Hannah visited Samuel annually, bringing him robes. This (in my opinion) was a tool Hannah used to build the foundation for Samuel. I can imagine young Samuel running errands in his robe. He looked different (in the outfit) from the other children. His mother must have been telling him, "My son, you are a priest. You are not like other children. You are different. You are separated unto the Lord. You are a precious gift from God." I can imagine Samuel asking all the *whys as children do today*. Why couldn't he wear jeans or other pants in vogue or a simple T-shirt like a regular child? Or just to wear an outfit that speaks to his generation and time? I want to believe the way he dressed as one of the tools his mother used to direct him on the way to his divine purpose—the priesthood.

The Builder. The Building. The Building Plan.

The Bible declares in Genesis 1:1, *"In the beginning, God created the heavens and the earth."* Our God is the Master Builder, the Builder of builders. He has the templates for life and living. When God created man, afterward, He breathed on him, and man became a living being. In Genesis 1:28, God gave man dominion over every living thing that moved upon the earth, including the things that were not physically present and yet to manifest. He gave us the mandate to build, tender, take care of, and nurture. Our children fall under this category that God mandated us to care for.

The Builder

From the above illustration, we can deduce that the God of Heaven has made us builders. We all are builders, irrespective of gender, status, or role! Using the analogy of a physical building, the type or model of the house you want will determine the resources you will need and how much commitment would be required. Many factors are essential in the building: environment, weather, economy, the builder's physical strength, knowledge of the subject matter, availability, and accessibility of natural supports, etc. The use or misuse of available resources or factors mentioned above will affect the overall turn out of the house. Although we have likened children to a house being built, they are not turnkey projects! They are given to us to start from scratch. Parents are literally likely to create the building blocks: lay them one by one on a rock-solid foundation already prepared.

The Building

In His words to us, Jesus Christ states, *"But don't begin until you count the cost. For who would begin construction of a building without first calculating the cost to see if there is enough money to finish it?"* (Luke 14:28 NLT).

The building, within the context of this book, is the child. Although we do not have to sit down to calculate how much it will cost us to care for a child from birth to adulthood (is there ever a time we will not be involved in their lives?). We do have a responsibility to consciously reflect on the necessary resources (spiritual, financial, emotional, or otherwise) required to give the child a fighting chance in the battles of life.

The Building Plan

The Bible declares in Joshua 1:8, *"Keep this Book of the Law always on your lips; meditate on it day and night, so that you may be careful to do everything written in it. Then you will be prosperous and successful.* (NIV).

17

The above Scripture makes us understand that no matter how good or anointed we are as builders or architects, we will always need a building plan. We need to have a well-documented and thought-out idea that will channel the course and fuel the direction we choose and anyone that comes along to work with us. Proverbs 22:6 (KJV) says when we *"Train up a child in the way he should go: and when he is old, he will not depart from it."* This is the template! Notice the emphasis on "the way he should go." The Bible states in John 14:6 that *"Jesus saith unto him, I am the way, the truth, and the life: no man cometh unto the Father, but by me."* (KJV).

Permit me to say that the way the child should go is the Jesus way. With the Bible as our guide, we as parents should always daily seek the face of God concerning our children, modeling Christian values.

When we have a clear understanding of our roles as builders, with a holistic approach to what we are building, and have equipped ourselves with the building plan (the Holy Bible), only then are we set to build!

The main aim of this book is to explore some of the various tools available to us as builders. As mentioned earlier, this is not to judge, stigmatize, or build stereotypes. The tools available to the builder are not limited to the ones mentioned in this book. As you read through, there are exercises at the end of each chapter that will help us explore and reflect on our feelings and thoughts. These exercises should not be brushed aside. You can also make a list of tools you are using, you have used, you have seen others use, or some new ones the Holy Spirit has ministered to you in the course of reading this book. Just picture a builder at a site. In building a physical structure, a tool is worthless in the worker's hand if he has no knowledge of its usage. This is the primary purpose of checking the manual (the Bible).

Every child is unique. Parenting is not a "buy one get one free" deal, and it is not a solo effort. The tools mentioned in this book work as a basis, and as the child grows, we begin to tailor the tools we have chosen to the age, stage, and uniqueness of the child. Each child is born with unique abilities and capabilities. In raising children, a specific strategy that had worked for one might not work for another child within the same family. There is a need to patiently explore and celebrate the uniqueness of each child and avoid comparison.

Prayers: The Foundational Tool

Prayer is the master key (tool), the foundational and fundamental tool. It brings about the effectiveness of other devices. Prayer is directly communicating with God. Prayer goes beyond just reciting our wish list before Him. The place of prayer is the place of fellowship and building a relationship—a two-way relationship. Prayer is our direct line of communication with God. Prayer is unique and never runs out of data, even when there are moments when we are so overwhelmed with the issues of life, questioning whether it is worth it. Prayer, as a spiritual resource, is what we should turn to, regularly and not just in a crisis like a 911 call. It is an expression of our faith in God as the Almighty: the admission of our human weaknesses and limitations. The Bible says, *"Therefore God exalted him to the highest place and gave him the name that is above every name, that at the name of Jesus every knee should bow, in heaven and on earth and under the earth"* Philippians 2:9-10 (NIV). We should pray in the name of Jesus.

The place of prayer is the place of receiving divine instructions, as King David made us understand that God has promised to instruct us and teach us in the way we should go and guide us with His eyes. The instructions needed to bring these precious gifts in the way of the Lord lies with us spending quality time with God in the place of prayer (see Psalms 32:8).

The Bible tells us, *"Never stop praying."* (1 Thessalonians 5:17 NLT). It means we are to do it at every moment, continually! There is generally no stipulated time or place for prayer. Prayer is a tool for building and a consequence of a relationship. But too often, people look at prayer as a place of last resort rather than a relationship. For practical reasons and for the sake of commitment and discipline, we can have a designated time and place to meet with God in prayers. Prayer is something that can and should be a part of our daily life by praying in the spirit as we go about our day. We can pray about everything and anything. Philippians 4:6 says, *"Do not be anxious about anything, but in every situation, by prayer and petition, with thanksgiving, present your requests to God."* (NIV). The types of requests and situation to present is not stated. Thus, it can mean we ought to present any and every request according to the will of God. This includes directions and instructions in building a solid spiritual foundation for our children.

God is compassionate. He answers prayers made in right standing with Him and according to His will and purpose for us. When it comes to answers to prayers, we all have different views and expectations of how we want our answered prayers to be delivered to us and when. For instance, we want it packaged and delivered in specific ways. But we should learn to trust God, including His way and timing for all things. In waiting for the physical manifestation of the answered prayers, wait in praise, in trust, and in faith. There might have been situations we have prayed about something. As situations unfold, we can become grateful that some prayers were not answered in the ways that we had initially hoped. There are also situations where the forces of darkness try to hinder what God has released. In Daniel, chapter 10, Daniel prayed, and for twenty-one days, his answer was delayed. After an angel was deployed to wrestle with the prince of Persia, then the answer was released.

As caregivers, there will be situations in which our children present challenges to our parental abilities, making us feel all our efforts are or have been in vain. We can feel like God is not answering our prayers. Trust me ... God answers your prayers! All we need to do is to keep praying and keep trusting, and we will see a beautiful building manifest to the glory of His name!

The major hindrance to this beautiful experience with God is sin. God is a faithful and Holy God. Isaiah 59:1-3 (NIV) gives a summary of the hindrances to prayers. *"Surely the arm of the Lord is not too short to save, nor his ear too dull to hear. But your iniquities have separated you from your God; your sins have hidden his face from you so that he will not hear. For your hands are stained with blood, your fingers with guilt. Your lips have spoken falsely, and your tongue mutters wicked things."* There is a turning point! Our God is merciful. He declared in Isaiah 1:18 (NLT), *"Come now, let us settle the matter,"* says the Lord. *"Though your sins be as scarlet, they shall be as white as snow; though they be as crimson, they shall be like wool."*

As we approach the throne of God in prayers, let us do so with clean hands and a pure heart, forgiving and knowing by faith that we are forgiven.

Co-Builders

As builders, we are not working alone; we have co-builders: other individuals involved in the child's life. School teachers, school bus drivers, instructors, family members—all have a part to play. How are we able to work together with other individuals involved in the life of the child to create a well-adjusted individual filled and operating under the direction of the Holy Spirit? Galatians 5:22 highlights the fruits of the Spirit.

Love

Joy

Peace

Gentleness

Goodness

Patience

Kindness

Faith

Self-Control

Reflecting on the definition of each fruit, a measure of each will come in handy in helping us build. These are virtues that will help us as builders. The grace for the manifestation of each fruit in our lives can be sought in the place of prayer.

Exercise

Explore the meaning of each fruit of the Spirit and summarize it in one word.

Love_____

Joy_____

Peace_____

Gentleness_____

Goodness_____

Patience_____

Kindness_____

Faith_____

Self-Control_____

Tool #1
Building the Foundation

I remember having limited access to books while growing up. My dad was an avid daily newspaper reader. We were introduced to this culture as soon as we could read. It then became something we looked forward to. We did the word search first and then read the cartoon section before reading the actual news.

Every child should be exposed to reading, especially the Bible, at a very early age. The parent should make every effort to graduate the child from being read to, to attempting to read, to reading aloud to parents and others. Then move on to learning to study the Bible. The Bible might not appear exciting to the child at first. The attending adult should come up with creative ways of making it appealing and not perceived as a punishment but as a means of building their spiritual database and knowing about God at an early stage and reading about His wonderful works. At the stage that the child is being read to, the child has no choice of the book. When the child gets to the level of reading by herself, the child can be given the option of the reading plan, thus making it an inclusive reading plan.

As a parent, coach, and a child development worker, I have had the opportunity to be at workshops, seminars, and webinars where, based on research work, reading has been discussed. The child does not need to read a whole book every day, but rather, is encouraged to commit dedicated time to read. The child should be encouraged to read aloud, paying close attention to proper pronunciation and punctuation, which will help the listener to spot any error and correct in love. Children are quick to fill in words they are unable to pronounce or understand. Listeners should encourage the child to read the actual words written in the book. For instance, saying *do not* instead of *do not* should be discouraged. Children should be interrupted intermittently and asked questions to determine their level of understanding of what they have been reading.

The habit or practice of daily reading is what should be developed and encouraged early in life. It is said in certain parts of the world that if you do not want people to have access to something or want to hide it, put it in a book. The information or knowledge will be kept safe since it is assumed that the people rarely read. This is where modeling comes to play. It is effortless for children to copy behaviors they observe us parents displaying over time. This can also apply to reading. If, as parents, we do not have great reading habits as part of our daily routine, it might be challenging to sit with our child and read to them or be read to. Reading within this context exceeds a child just meeting deadlines with homework.

In addition to the Bible and other spiritual materials, children should be exposed to age-appropriate, character building, and educational books. As much as reading should be fun, there should be life lessons and positive applicable skills to learn after reading a book. Parents should guide children in their choice of books.

In the summer of 2016, I wanted to get some books for my daughter from the library. To my utmost surprise, most of the chapter books were fictional about dragons, witches, wizards, magic, and the like. Do not get me wrong. I do not have anything against fiction books. My concern is the limited access to spiritual books and books that teach life skills and encourage critical thinking and problem-solving skills for children? Why is it that our libraries are short on faith-based literature and materials? One of the librarians answered the question, but all I could summarize from her answer was that they lacked funding. There is the adage: "He who pays the piper dictates the tune." The funders project their ideology into the children's minds, thus "catching them young." This calls for the church as a whole to be sensitive and respond to this need! At this point, the spiritual leaders should rise up to their apparent social responsibility and supply libraries and schools with books and materials that teach about salvation and the knowledge of Christ as early as possible.

The second answer I got to my question was given by Nifemi Aborowa, a soft-spoken ten-year-old. His response was, "But auntie, where can we get those books? We read the books we find in the library and the schools. And at times, the books are scary." Let us, as caregivers, invest in books for our children.

The importance of reading cannot be overemphasized. According to a study by the Fisher Centre for Alzheimer's Research Foundation, "reading has been identified to help protect and increase memory" and "help with the overall brain function." Other benefits of reading include but are not limited to vocabulary expansion, improved focus, good writing and thinking skills, and increased improvement in concentration. Reading has been referred to "as a good workout" for the brain. Below are a few examples of the importance of reading.

The Importance of Reading

Vocabulary Expansion

The more a child reads, the more words he or she is exposed to. According to TeachHUB, "Vocabulary is the knowledge of words and their meanings."[2] The knowledge of words helps the child to have an extensive "word bank." One of the many ways to improve our vocabulary is consistent and committed reading of age-appropriate literature. As they are exposed to new words, they are encouraged to find meanings from the books, forming sentences to show their full understanding.

Improved Focus

Getting a child to concentrate and focus on an activity for X amount of time can be an arduous task. They are active, energetic, curious, and little explorers in their cute little ways. But, you cannot read on the go, so you need to sit them down to concentrate. That is why reading is one of the many ways to improve their ability to focus. By teaching and encouraging them to focus through reading, they learn to develop skills that deal with distractions and learning to focus on one thing at a time. Parents and caregivers also need to exhibit a high level of focus. They should put aside anything that might constitute a distraction to both parties such as cell phones, tablets, cooking, or even doing light household chores on the side, and the like.

Pace should also be considered, especially when the child gets to the age of reading chapter books. If one chapter per day is all the child can do, that should be respected and increased as time goes on. I did this with my daughter. We read alternate pages, and we do not read more than one chapter per night, or we take turns reading a paragraph each to make it a fun learning experience. When we read the Bible, if it is one of the genealogies, I read it to prevent her from losing interest.

This time should be cherished and valued by parents. Besides promoting increased focus for the child, it also allows parents and caregivers to bond with children. Children are mostly visual learners. Age-appropriate, exciting, and colorful books will quickly catch the attention of the child.

Critical Thinking Skills

Critical thinking is thinking clearly about what to do based on the information at hand. With daily exposure to books, children are exposed to many opportunities to develop and practice these skills.

Creative Thinking Skills

According to the online business dictionary, creative thinking is "the ability to look at situations or scenarios from a fresh perspective." Creative thinking gives children the ability to think outside the box. For instance, reading through the story of Joseph in Genesis 37, a child could be asked what he thinks Joseph could have done differently, or if he were Joseph, what he would have done. Writing and rewriting the story's ending is an excellent way to stimulate this process and expand their creative thinking skills.

Developing A Reading Culture

The Bible states in Roman 10:17 (KJV) that faith *"cometh by hearing, and hearing by the word of God."* This should not be limited to a message from the pulpit. The more a child is exposed to Christian literature, the more knowledge and understanding of God that child will have, gradually building up their faith. This knowledge will help the child navigate through life. Everything in life needs to be built, including a reading habit. Any habit we want to see in our child should be seen displayed in us first.

I read a story of a young boy going away on a journey. His mother gave him a Bible, so that each time he needed money, or his resources were depleted, he should open to Philippians 4:19. This was not the case for this individual; even with little or no support, he did not open his Bible to read. Years after, according to the narrative, he picked up his Bible, although not to read, then a note fell out of it. The message on the note instructed him on how to get money should his resources ever run low.

I cannot verify the authenticity of the story. Still, if this individual had come from a home where a reading culture was cultivated, he might have missed how he used to read with his mother, or the urge to read would be strong. As parents and caregivers, let us practice developing and maintaining a reading culture. The Bible declares in Proverbs 22:6 to *"train up a child in the way he should go, and when he is old, he will not depart from it."* That training can come from them just doing what they see us do. Let us model reading to our children.

Committed Daily Reading

It is advised to introduce children to reading age-appropriate literature. But with easy access to electronic gadgets, it is harder for children to develop a committed, daily reading habit without distractions. Ongoing research has shown that reading e-books with children are not as helpful to both parties as reading a print book. According to a write-up, researchers from the University of Michigan carried out a research on thirty-seven parents and their toddlers. During this research, parents and children were observed reading printed books, e-books on tablets, and advanced e-books with sound effects and animations. The study showed that with electronic gadgets, there were many distractions as the parents focused more on controlling the child fiddling with the device rather than on the reading exercise. According to the article, Dr. Tiffany Munzer stated: "Parents interact less when reading electronic books together than printed ones."[3] She also mentioned that reading with or to your child promotes "language development, literacy and bonding" and that "while many of the interactions between parents and young children may appear subtle, they were important in promoting healthy child development." According to the study, parents who use e-books were advised to consider exploring print books and their associated benefits. Reading books in print, as opposed to e-books, allows the parents to bond because of the interaction, closeness, and open-ended conversations between mother and child.

Technology in and of itself is not bad; its abuse creates concerns for parents and caregivers alike. Committed, daily reading can be as little as thirty minutes a day or a chapter per day. Commitment on the part of the parent is the most essential tool here. I have caught myself straying a couple of times from this plan. I do not go on a blame game. I just pick up where I left.

Mentoring vs. Monitoring

"The key to being a good mentor is to help people become more of who they are —not make them more like you."
Suze Orman[4]

When we think of a mentor, what usually comes to mind is someone else whom our child or children want to emulate. Or an individual we desire to mentor our child to become the person we want them to be. We often do not give it a thought to mentor our children ourselves to help them be themselves. According to Wikipedia, "Mentorship is a relationship in which a more experienced or more knowledgeable person helps to guide a less experienced or less knowledgeable person. The mentor may be older or younger than the person being mentored, but he or she must have certain experience in the area of expertise."[5]

As caregivers, we need to prayerfully guide and guard our children. As mentoring caregivers, we should be good examples. It is easier for them to copy what we do than do what we tell them to do. I carried out a self-directed experiment a while ago in my church. During a mid-week service, it was a bit challenging to get the under-fives to sit down. After some failed attempts at getting them to sit and not run around, I went to a corner and sat down. Surprisingly, one after the other, they all came and sat by my side. A sister in the church noticed this and took a picture. They sat because I was sitting.

When I was growing up, I noticed we had to sweep the house religiously at 4 p.m. every day. No matter how clean the house looked, smelled, or felt—we had to sweep! The only reason we could deduce for this was that my father gets home from work at about 4:30 p.m., so the house should be clean. After I got married, I found myself doing the same; no matter how clean the place was, I had to sweep and clean by 4 p.m.! I developed this habit because this was what I had seen my mom do. I grew into this; it became a part of me, and I carried it into adulthood.

As adults, we should be more aware of our actions because the little ones are watching and learning. We can actually be that mentor we are looking for to mentor them.

Exercise

In the last 12 months, how many books have you read? Please list them here.

_____

_____

_____

As a child growing up, who was your mentor?

_____

_____

_____

What were the qualities you saw in your mentor?

_____

_____

_____

Who is your child's mentor? (You can ask him or her and please do not feel bad if you do not appear on their list)

_____

_____

_____

On a scale of 0- 10, how comfortable are you with mentoring your child/ren? 0 – Lowest 10 – Highest

_____

In what area or areas do you think you can mentor your child/ren more?

_____

_____

_____

As mentioned earlier, the exercises in the book are not there to judge anyone's parenting skills, but rather to get us thinking about those areas we want to improve on. It might merely be to give us a different perspective on issues. No parent is perfect, and no child is perfect either. We all want the best for our children, and we want them to integrate well into society, pleasing God in all they do.

Tool #2
Building Options

*S*ee, today I appoint you over nations and kingdoms to uproot and *tear down, to destroy and overthrow, to build and to plant."* (Jeremiah 1:10 NIV).

From the above Scripture, the Lord has appointed us to uproot, tear down, destroy, and overthrow. The verse did not end there, because we are to build and plant. Our God is not the God of a vacuum! After we have uprooted, what are we building in the vacant space? Jesus told a parable about a man from whom demons were chased away, and the place swept clean. Mathew 12:43-45 says, *"When the unclean spirit is gone out of a man, he walketh through dry places, seeking rest, and findeth none. Then he saith, I will return unto my house from whence I came out; and when he is come, he findeth it empty, swept, and garnished. Then goeth he, and taketh with himself seven other spirits more wicked than himself, and they enter in and dwell there: and the last state of that man is worse than the first. Even so, shall it be also unto this wicked generation"* (KJV).

From the above Scriptures, the evil spirits had gone out of the man, but nothing occupied the empty space. When they came back, it was "empty, swept, and garnished." As caregivers, we should not create vacuums in the lives of our children. When we take something from them, what are we replacing it with? This chapter looks into the importance of not creating that vacuum.

Creating a Vacuum

Providing, promoting, and encouraging healthy eating habits are most dear to every caring caregiver's heart. Providing our children with food rich in vitamins and nutrients and discouraging junk food should be paramount. As we care about the physical and mental well-being of our children, the same, if not higher, attention and effort should be paid to their spiritual diet and well-being as well.

Often as parents, we are quick to instruct children on what literature not to read, what not to wear, what kind of music not to listen to, what kind of games not to play. Often, this only creates a void in the lives of children. No alternative is given. In our Bible text, we are encouraged to uproot and build, thereby not creating a vacuum.

Currently, more attention is given to getting the child to eat healthy meals. We often will want to stock the house with fruits and veggies as opposed to junk. In so doing, we are making sure the child has easy access to healthy food. There is the saying that "an apple a day keeps the doctor away."[6] In the same way, one chapter of the Bible a day keeps the devil away (my version).

What are the healthy options we are making available for our children? What healthy spiritual options can we provide for them? Or are we providing for them? What type of literature populates our homes? What type of music are these children exposed to? What apps do they have on their gadgets? These innocent ones have these items in their possession because these are usually what they have access to. As builders and caregivers, we are to offer to those in our care food, technology, and literature that will build up their faith and help them become responsible, caring adults. We need to extend this from eating organic foods and living a healthy lifestyle, to spiritual choices and tools that will build up their spiritual lives.

In the previous chapter, we compared building the child to building a physical structure. I want to believe that no builder would want to skimp on resources and compromise the end product. The same should apply to building a solid spiritual foundation for our children. Children are very visual; they would prefer a colorful, appealing product even though it might not be beneficial to them in the end. They lack the discernment to see the harm that could result. Often, I hear parents talk about a lack of access to spiritual materials. Still, we are in a digital world now. We live in a global village. We can get anything we want from the comfort of our homes on the Internet. No more excuses! As parents, we need to think outside the box and begin to make conscious efforts to provide access to spiritually sound and fun resources for our children.

The Fun Stuff

Children like to have fun while learning because they get bored quickly, and their attention spans can be quite limited. According to *Day 2 Day Parenting*,[7] "The attention span for children between ages 5 and 6 is between 10 to 15 minutes while older children between ages 6 and 7 can hold up an activity for up to 30 minutes." When children are actively engaged in fun, creative, open-ended activities that can help with their creative thinking and problem-solving skills, they often feel more motivated to engage for more extended periods. This could most likely be why children spend long hours on gadgets playing games. There are many fun spiritual materials out there that can keep the children engaged and build them up spiritually. The first and best of this, as mentioned earlier, is the Bible. Reading a chapter a day will not make it tedious, and one can follow up with relevant short videos. With this, they will still have access to the constructive use of technology. Also available are Bible fun games, puzzles, word searches, and trivia. There are Bible apps available to meet this need.

Technology, Your Child, and You

Katherine Lee, in her write-up on "The Concerns About Kids and Screen Time: What research says about the impact on health and development,"[8] she revealed that the usage of technology for children is not limited to their exposure to it at a very young age but "they are also using it in more situations, both at home and at school." She also stated that "perhaps parents having a better understanding of where experts' recommendations come from (research) may help them decide what limits they might want to set at home when it comes to screen time."

There has been a lot of debate about the effects of screen time, cognitive development of children, and the duration of screen time. According to a study published in *The Lancet Child and Adolescent Health Journal*,[9] "Screen time for a child in whatever form, be it that it requires focus or not, or mainly for entertainment or educational purposes can affect a child's cognitive functioning and development. Children are being advised to engage in at least one hour of physical activity, get between nine to eleven hours of sleep, and not more than two hours of screen time."

A longitudinal study[10] was carried out in 2016. A total of 4,524 children between the ages of eight to eleven were observed. The three areas of study were screen time, physical activity, and sleep. Questionnaires were completed by both parents and children at the beginning of the study to measure typical behaviors in these three domains.

The findings of this study showed a significant number of children did not meet any of the three recommended guidelines. The results showed 30 percent did not meet any of the three, a little over 40 percent met one, and 25 percent met two, while 5 percent met all three recommendations. This research was carried out between September 2016 and September 2017. This translates to a conclusion that most of the children were not getting enough sleep. They were not engaged in at least an hour of daily physical activity and were engaging in screen time for more than an hour each day.

According to an article written by Kimberly Young, a guest author on "Children and Technology: Parent guidelines for every age" in the Society on Social implication and Technology web page: "The time a child spends on any form of gadgets, be it television, tablet, laptop, or desktop should be age-appropriate." According to Kimberly, "Children need different rules at different ages of development."[11]

Here are the 3-6-9-12 rules for the home, which parents may want to consider in determining how much technology their child should be exposed to.

The table below highlights her point.

Age	Recommendation
Birth to 3 years	Never or none (Surprised?)
3 to 6 years	One hour a day
6 to 9 years	Two hours a day Active supervision is required, still limited to two hours a day.
9 to 12 years	Responsible use This is relative. But it is still advised not more than two hours a day.
12 to 18 years	Independent use

How easy is it to comply with these guidelines in today's society? A twelve-month-old child can identify the YouTube icon before knowing her shapes and colors. Navigating through any form of device is no longer the challenge. This is a cause for concern and calls for prayers and hard work on parents and caregivers. The duration is what can be discussed amongst all concerned. I remember when my youngest child was little. I had a discussion with her about the amount of time she spends on devices, so she understood. We explored options for using her one hour; we eventually agreed at thirty minutes each twice a day. We also decided each session should be at least three hours apart. This worked well for a couple of years until we had to revisit it because of her schoolwork.

As parents, we are mostly good at handing down instructions, which is not to say we should not be assertive. We should often explore the chances of offering options and guiding them to make the right decision. Joshua 24:15 (NIV) reads, *"But if serving the Lord seems undesirable to you, then choose for yourselves this day whom you will serve, whether the gods your ancestors served beyond the Euphrates or the gods of the Amorites, in whose land you are living. But as for me and my household, we will serve the Lord."* Also, Deuteronomy 30:15 (NIV) states, *"See, I set before you today life and prosperity, death and destruction."* These two leaders (Joshua and Moses, respectively) made options available to the children of Israel. Still, they guided them in making the right decision within the available options. We are also at a time where homework can be accessed online; this makes the child an easy target for distraction.

Though it might be hard to follow the 3-6-9-12 rule, supervision at every stage is required. Various research studies are still ongoing concerning the impact of technology on children. Let us, as caregivers, in whatever capacity, stay connected and be in the know of the latest research findings and be able to use such results to guide our children. I want to see technology as a blessing and not a curse.

Technology: A Way out for Parents?

Offering the children a tablet or phone is our easiest route out of any behavior we are not able or ready to deal with at any particular point in time. At times, we just want to keep them quiet while we go about our chores. Let us always remember the 3-6-9-12 rule.

While we take or plan to take technology from the children, what healthy alternative choices are we offering? Are we offering healthy, spiritual, educative, fun items that will build their spirits, souls, and bodies? As mentioned earlier, we do not want to intentionally create a vacuum.

No caregiver will subject their children to malnourishment, so we put in efforts to provide healthy meals. We should also guide our children from suffering from spiritual malnutrition. Malnutrition, according to the online dictionary, is "the unhealthy condition that results from not eating enough food or not eating enough healthy food."[12]

The addiction to technology, in my opinion, is a habit that was created and nurtured by most of us. At a child's tender age, we place them directly in front of the television to focus on our task genuinely and sincerely for the day and check off our to-do list. We are happy the child is doing so well, quiet, and gentle, but this child sits endlessly in front of the television. I was caught in that web too. I want to get things done fast and uninterrupted. I needed to find a means to get my son to settle down, and technology came to my rescue! Would I have done things differently if given another chance? Yes! This is what I regard as the days of the unknown, but the Bible tells us, *"we have no excuse"* (See Romans 2:1).

Protecting Children Online

Internet Safety

Technology is one of God's many blessings to mankind. Technology has made the world a global village. With the invention of phones and other electronic gadgets, an individual can travel the world in the palm of their hand. They can shop and be conversant with all that is going on worldwide, from the comfort of their own private space. This freedom is what God has blessed humanity with.

How, then, can we make our children safe in this "global village"? Our children need to connect with the outside world, either to get homework done or for leisure. There is a need to make this a simple, secure, safe, and fun experience for our children due to associated risk, no matter the age of the child. There have been so many cases of cyberbullying and predators disguised as children to lure children into disclosing personal information and other things.

As parents, we should be conversant with Internet laws. We should have open conversations with our children regarding such and be aware of what our children are exposed to online. There is a need for our children to be schooled in responsible Internet manners and let them know the basic guidelines for safe use, so their safety and that of families and friends are not jeopardized.

According to KidsHealth.org, on Internet safety, "Children should be encouraged not to share private personal information such as location, names, phone numbers, exchange pictures, or share passwords other than with their parents. Children should not agree to meet face to pace with anyone they meet online without the knowledge and express consent and approval of the parent."[13] As parents, we should strive to develop and maintain a healthy relationship with our children. Make them comfortable having conversations with us around any uncomfortable or uneasy discussions they might have stumble on or having with anyone over the Internet.

KidsHealth also encouraged parents to spend time with the children online and teach them "appropriate online behaviors." It is also encouraged to place the computer in a common area where "favorites and frequently visited websites are bookmarked" for easy access. Parents are also encouraged to check their credit cards and phone bills for any suspicious activity on their accounts. Children should be taken seriously if they report suspicious online activity.

Below are the signs highlighted on KidsHealth, which might indicate when a child is the target of an online predator. They are but not limited to:

- spending long hours online, especially at night
- phone calls from people you do not know
- unsolicited gifts arriving in the mail
- your child suddenly turning off the computer when you walk into the room
- withdrawal from family life and reluctance to discuss online activities

The law also prohibits a site from requiring a child to provide more personal information than necessary to play a game or enter a contest. The children are in a hurry to play their game, and they might not want to put in the time to ask an adult for consent. Children are also smart enough to fake information about themselves, such as a minor presenting as an adult.

Online Protection Tools

Online tools let us control our kids' access to adult material and help protect them from Internet predators. Many Internet Service Providers (ISPs) provide parent-control options. We can also obtain or subscribe to a software that helps block access to sites and restricts personal information from being sent online. Other programs can monitor and track online activity.

Page Content

The Internet is a dangerous place for children and teens. Online safety is so important to help keep our children safe. If we, as parents, are not vigilant or up to date with the available safety tools, how can we be prepared to help our children understand the dangers, address them, and keep them safe? Their safety should be our priority!

If you observe child abuse or child pornography on the Internet, please report it immediately to Cybertip.ca. Cybertip will then forward the information to the regional policing agency to investigate. You can include images that you think may have occurred outside of your home province and Canada.

Some societies might not have as many resources as others. Still, when we resolve to seek out, we might find some resources to help our children.

Below are some tips to help keep your children safe online. These tips are not *one size fits all*. Some factors can make or mar the effectiveness of whatever tip or tips you want to engage in: the age of the child or children, the family, the makeup, and the social-economic status (in some households, everyone has free access to one form of gadget or the other, in other homes, this may not be the case).

- Maintain open lines of communication between parents and children.

- Make sure they know that they should never, under any circumstances, reveal *any* personal information over the Internet, whether in chat rooms, surveys or on websites.
- They must never agree to meet in person an individual they met on the Internet.
- Teach children to stop using the Internet immediately and advise parents if they see or read anything that upsets them.
- Keep your computer with Internet access in a high traffic area of the home.
- Restrict access to the Internet when there is no supervision available.
- Sign an Internet family contract with all Internet users within the home.
- Select a family-friendly Internet Service Provider (ISP). Some ISP's offer guidelines for parents. They provide support in setting up parental control features, provide kids-only areas, block child pornography from their newsgroup servers, help find interesting kid sites on the Internet, and respond quickly to reports of online abuse. Others leave these issues up to parents to figure out on their own.
- Use protective software, including anti-virus and firewall protection. Research the use of parental monitoring software in certain circumstances.
- Parents should take a course on the use of the Internet or have their child teach them. Make it a fun, creative, family activity.
- Have ongoing conversations with the children on the subject matter.

Ways to Limit Technology

Katherine Lee stated that "letting kids use technology with limits can be achieved if you keep some of these key tips in mind." Below are the tips suggested in her write-up "Ways to Limit Technology."[14]

- Do not put a TV in your child's room. Having a TV in their bedroom has been linked to several problems, including lower test scores, sleeping problems, and obesity.
- Turn it off. When the kids are not watching a specific program, turn off the television. Keep it off during mealtimes and especially when they are studying or doing homework.
- Help your child choose a video game or a show. The best way to know what your child is watching or playing is by helping them pick it out. When picking out a new family movie or game, read the reviews, watch previews, or ask other parents. Above all, know your child and trust your own instincts on what is appropriate.
- Place time limits. Whether it is one hour of TV and/or video games a day or a couple of hours a week, limit the amount of time your child spends with technology. More importantly, be committed and stick to those times you set.
- Opt for alternatives to technology-based activities. Find great ways to spend family time together without tech devices, such as playing board games or enjoying the outdoors.
- Have a weekly tech-free day: All family members agree on a day of the week to be free of technology. Parents might be the ones to struggle with this. It might not be for the whole day; it can be for some hours in the morning or afternoon. No matter the time that works for the family, be sure to have a plan in place, so you are not caught in the trap of 'I am bored!'

The Internet and Teens

As children get older, it gets a little more challenging to monitor their activities online. Most teenagers are more knowledgeable about the Internet at this stage than most adults. Most, if not all, have unlimited access to devices. This is the independent stage, where children will need some form of independence from their parents to explore their world. They will want to make some new connections and maintain old ones. It might appear complicated, but it could be rewarding to continually have open conversations with our teenagers about safe and healthy Internet habits. Educate them about boundaries and the need to protect their passwords, thus protecting themselves against identity theft. Parents need to have conversations with them about the dangers of interacting with strangers online and play an active role in ensuring they benefit from their Internet experience.

In her article "Parenting the Video Game Fanatic: How to encourage other interests" in Calgary's *Child Magazine*, Cheryl Maguire encourages parents to create boundaries and "learn more about their teen's interest in video games. Sit down with them and play the game with them."[15] This will help you understand their interest and have some healthy conversations about the subject matter.

To avoid creating a vacuum as parents, guardians, and caregivers, we need to fill in the gap of time for our children. But with what? Some of us might ask. Our children have so much energy that needs to be channeled appropriately. They are mighty arrows that should be shot in the right direction (See Psalms 127: 3-5).

Now that we have imbibed the 3-6-9-12 rules, which might not be as easy as it sounds, clear and simple communication of expectations with everyone is essential. I have heard about some family rules that state, "no television during the school week, the school week is for homework," etc. What about schools that do not assign homework to the child? What happens during the weekend? These are some questions to explore. The answers lie within several factors, such as the family dynamics, the physical environment, the physical and mental health of all involved in the life of the child, age, physical and psychological development, and so on. Dr. Larry D. Rosen was quoted in the same article by Cheryl Maguire, encouraging parents to "avoid announcing which activities their teens must do."[16] He expresses the need to involve the child in the decision-making as earlier mentioned.

There are some habits highlighted by Cheryl Maguire that, as parents, should be a cause of concern if we see our teens displaying them. Some of these traits might be shown in an Autistic child and not necessarily be unhealthy because of how they focus on and process the world. Still, generally speaking for our teens, they are as follows:

- Isolating behavior or ignoring family and friends
- Sneaking games to play at night or at a friend's house
- (Negative) changes in eating or sleeping patterns
- Decline in academic performance or not doing homework
- A need to continue playing video games beyond a specific time limit
- An interest only in playing video games at the expense of other activities
- Always thinking about video games

This is not a point to be judgmental, but rather to rise up prayerfully and find ways to support the child.

Developing Recreation Habits

The Bible declares in 1 Timothy 4:8A (KJV), *"For bodily exercise profiteth little."* That little profit that bodily exercise provides is worth exploring and gaining.

There is a need to develop recreational habits. Most of our children are in sports, but these are mostly instructional or competitive sports. Recreation is defined by the Mariam-Webster Learners dictionary as "something people do to relax or have fun: activities are done for enjoyment."[17] There are community-based recreational activities that families can engage in, such as meeting new people, making new friends, being actively involved in the community, socializing, and enjoying the cultural and physical activities the community has to offer.

Developing recreational habits help to get us moving and doing. If we, as caregivers, do not see any benefit in being engaged in recreational activities, either individually or as a family, we are less likely to promote this in our children. There are ongoing talks about risky play and the need for the child to move. Risky play is outdoor play whereby the child is exposed to a level of guided risk. The "risk" might involve playing with tools that ordinarily the child would not be exposed to, i.e., heights, speed. etc. This will be an incidental teaching moment for us as parents and caregivers to help children understand taking risks, problem-solving, self-regulation, and resilience. Children also experience immediate and direct consequences of their actions and can make informed decisions. Also, the age and development of the child should be considered. At the same time, adequate supervision and support are provided every step of the way. The word of God declared in Psalms 32:8-9 (NIV) says, *"I will instruct you and teach you in the way you should go; I will counsel you with my loving eye on you. Do not be like the horse or the mule, which have no understanding but must be controlled by bit and bridle or* they *will not come to you."* If our Lord and Savior have made a covenant to watch over us and not let us go as we engage in the *risky play* of life, how much more should we *instruct, teach, and counsel* the children he has given us (either spiritual or biological)? That they will not be like they who *have no understanding* but "must be controlled by bit and bridle" before they can understand or follow through with instructions.

Parents need to seek out free or subsidized recreational activities within their communities. There are programs and initiatives around Canada for those living in this part of the world who help support recreational activities. For some of us who have no access to free or subsidized recreational activities, we need to think outside the box. The end goal is to employ every tool within our disposal to build a complete child: Spirit, Soul, and Body! Taking a walk to the park, a bike ride, going swimming, etc. are some free activities to explore. Some organizations provide sports gear for free; some give some form of funding to a certain amount. A known initiative in Alberta is the Grade 6 YMCA free recreation pass for the whole school year. This is amazing, and it is worth exploring. Rather than having sedentary activities, you can take a trip to the library, park, or other recreational venues. No matter what part of the world we live in, we should look beyond our immediate environment, think outside the box, and get moving and active with our children.

Knowing the Whys

Humans are generally inquisitive, but children are even more so. They will always want to know why? *Why* should I spend only two hours on my game, TV, or tablet? *Why* do I have to go for a walk? *Why* do I have to have X number of hours of sleep? *Why* do I have to read a chapter of the Bible a day? It is endless! As much as these questions might appear irritating, let us begin to see them as innocent questions from a child who really wants to know. Let us take time to explain to them in simple and understandable terms the reasons for the tasks. I totally agree that this might generate more "whys." But from personal experience, the why decreases after some time. At this stage, children have learned that mummy or daddy or the caregiver will always have a reason for doing the task.

Moreover, most of the task is being undertaken together with the child. Both parties are benefiting. The Bible made us understand that *"And the Lord turned the captivity of Job when he prayed for his friends: also, the Lord gave Job twice as much as he had before."* (Job 42:10 KJV). As we undertake these activities with our children, we are equally benefiting. As we build, the building and the builders are both beneficiaries of the great work.

There are research-based answers to most of these innocent questions; let us take time to search them out and put them in simple terms for our children. We could also pull out short animation videos that would explain the whys and not just because mummy said so! For instance, a three-minute animation video of the importance of sleep to the brain or the significance of the physical activity to the body will go a long way in answering the why questions.

As we encourage or put strategies in place for our children to have less technology time, we as parents should be role models when it comes to usage of technology and limit our social use time as well. This does not apply to parents whose primary job is working with technology. We should think outside the box and have "no-tech centred activities for the entire family."

As builders, we receive grace to build according to the pattern, like Solomon built the temple. In Jesus' name.

Exercise

Which of the Online Safety Resources are you willing to try out?

_____

_____

_____

_____

_____

Which of the ways to limit technology are you willing to explore? When is your start date?

_____

_____

_____

_____

_____

Also, do find time to evaluate your commitment to the above listed.

Screen Time Exercise

I am concerned about my child's/ren's screen time usage
YES/ NO/ NOT SURE

List the present concerned behaviors you can see.

_____

_____

_____

_____

Ways to support my child/ren

_____

_____

_____

_____

Strategies to put in place

_____

_____

_____

_____

(Do not forget The Foundational Tool - Prayers)

Tool #3
Building Investments

Parenting can be energy-sapping, and at the same time, exciting, fun, and rewarding. From previous chapters, we can deduce that there is a tremendous amount of work put in by the caregivers. None of the tools mentioned in the earlier chapters will yield meaningful, long-lasting results without the conscious, intentional investment of our time and financial resources. Either or both of the tools mentioned in this chapter, when applied appropriately, sandwiched with prayers, will (by His grace) yield meaningful results.

As mentioned previously, the way of Jesus is the way to go. The training here requires teaching, constant encouragement, and modeling of high moral standards and spiritual values. The more quality, attentive time spent with our children, the more we can unconsciously influence their outlook on and interpretation of life.

In Deuteronomy 6:7 (KJV), Moses said, *"And thou shalt teach them diligently to thy children, and shalt talk of them when thou sittest in thine house, and when though liest down, and* when *thou risest up."* This command does not sound like an easy one, but it sure is worth investing time and money. Teaching is not a one-off. The above Scripture admonishes us to talk to our children when we sit, lie down, and rise up. In summary, it tells us to teach them continually "in thine house." This can translate to the simple understanding that the teaching should be done by me, at my house. It is not and should not be a delegated responsibility. There might be some overwhelming times and situations where we need external help and support, but this does not relieve us of the primary responsibility.

According to the Cambridge Dictionary, *diligent* means to be "careful and using a lot of effort" and for things to be "done in a careful and detailed way."[18] Diligent also means "steady, earnest, and energetic effort, and it is painstaking." And it is "constant in effort to accomplish something" and being "attentive and persistent in doing anything."

From the three definitions, I summarize being diligent as putting in the effort to do things carefully and accomplish a goal. No matter what you are trying to build, be it a house, a business, a career, a family, or a marriage. Everything in life requires putting effort and resources together to start up (a foundation)!

This is what the Lord expects of us all. We should consciously make time to teach and talk to our children. What do we teach them? What do we speak to them? We teach and talk to them about God, His mightiness, His love, His grace, and His word! We talk to them about morals, values, and life skills diligently. This should be done "when thou sittest in thine house." This does not mean teachings should only happen at home. There is room for incidental teachings.

Incidental teaching is when a child asks a question. The caregiver uses that as an opportunity to offer advice on the subject. Sitting, in this context, can be associated with calmness, concentration, and connection between everyone involved.

Investment of Time

As caregivers, we often get so caught up with actualizing our life goals that we gradually and unconsciously neglect the main reason why we are called parents or caregivers.

Time is defined as "the measured or measurable period during which an action, process, or condition exists or continues (*Merriam-Webster Collegiate Dictionary*[19]). One interesting fact about time is that it cannot be regained once it is lost. The moral lesson here is that we should spend it wisely.

As parents, we are daily wrapped up in the business of life, actualizing our own goals, and wearing many hats, yet we still want to remain sane and not stressed out. Life is hectic, I will not have enough time, and twenty-four hours will never be enough to do everything that needs to be done.

The investment of time is not limited to spending time with the children. It could also involve the time spent as parents to look for creative ways to spend time with them and keep them actively engaged and productive.

Children grow up incredibly fast, and parenting is a lifelong career! Our active engagement in their lives can be for a short time, but the teachings and values that have been instilled in their lives is eternal! So, building them for eternity by building a solid spiritual foundation for our children is worth it.

It is important to note that we cannot sit our children down and teach them everything they need to know in life. Some things can only be communicated in a nonverbal fashion. They watch us live and go about our lives. We are sometimes the book they read. Children are likely to mirror their behavior after someone they spend the most time with. It is necessary for us as an adult to model good and Godly behaviors and values.

Whenever possible, consider the schedule of all involved. Families need to agree on a weekly time together, one which every family member is committed to. For instance, every Friday from 7 p.m. to 9 p.m., consider the work schedules of adults in the family and, of course, the children's school and extracurricular activities. In a situation where one parent works a night shift, the dynamics will be different. Spending quality time with our children should be treasured. At these designated times, we should be fully attentive to our children and not divide our attention and time with electronic gadgets!

Spending time with our children and family members helps build stronger relationships and beautiful, pleasant memories. My family and I were having our "family meeting" some time ago. My children could remember some fun places and times we have spent together. The Holy Spirit whispered to me that these children could not remember the clothes, the shoes, the restaurants we have been to. They did make mention of some, but what they remembered most was our time together!

Spending time with our children, either individually or collectively, helps us understand each child's uniqueness. We can identify their strengths and weaknesses, and we can support them with the needed resources and, of course, through the word of God. We are their safety nets. They can feel comfortable enough to have conversations with us. This does not just happen; it takes time, work, and effort. As caregivers, we will prefer our children to talk to us and getting the right counsel from us or other trusted adults rather than strangers. It is imperative to know that the person speaking into our lives influences our decisions in life.

In 2 Chronicles, Chapter 10, the Bible gave an account of King Jeroboam. He reigned after the death of his father, King Solomon. The people of the land came to appeal to his conscience to make their burden lighter. The king requested three days to think about their request. The king then consulted the elders and the wise men who served during the reign of his father. Their response in 2 Chronicles 10:7 was *"If thou be kind to this people, and please them, and speak to them, they will be thy servants forever."* (KJV). The king did not take the advice of the elders. He then turned to seek counsel from the young men, and they advised him to tell the people *that "My little finger shall be thicker than my father's loins. For whereas my father put a heavy yoke upon you, I will put more to your yoke: my father chastised you with whips, but I will chastise you with scorpions."* (2 Chronicles 10:10-11).

The people we interact with and the relationships we form play a considerable part in the actualization of our goals in life. We cannot be with our children twenty-four hours a day. but by building a healthy relationship with them, we can be their safety nets. They can check in with us regarding significant milestone decisions. We are also able to model good relationships and help them build their self-esteem. They are encouraged to believe in themselves, the choices they make in life, and to live a life of accountability.

Quality time does not necessarily mean a huge chunk of time. It can be as little as thirty minutes of daily reading or a trip to the grocery store. We should bear in mind that, as caregivers, we need time to check in with ourselves. We would not want to burn out or be stressed out. We can take care of members of our families and those around us, only if we are strong and able to do so. We need to take time out of our busy schedule to take care of ourselves. This is called "self-care."

Self-care is a practice we are encouraged to add to our daily routine to prevent us from burnout to effectively build. I have often been caught in the web of believing self-care is a waste of time, or it is the "selfish side" of me manifesting itself. I have long since realized that there will always be something or someone to attend to outside of me, but I am responsible for me. I am the only person who can take care of myself. There are many affordable and free self-care activities to engage in. All you need to do is figure out what works for you in terms of your schedules and budget, and then commit to it.

Katherine Hurst, the founder of The Law of Attraction Community, describes self-care as "anything you do to be good to yourself. It is partly knowing when your resources are running low and stepping back to replenish them rather than letting them all drain away. When practiced correctly, self-care has long-term benefits for the mind, body, or both."[20]

She also highlights the top five benefits of self-care.

1. *Better productivity:* self-care helps to "slow down life in a wonderful way."

2. *Improved resistance to diseases:* self-care helps the body to go "into a restful, rejuvenating mode, helping it to fortify its immune system. So, with better self-care comes fewer colds, cases of flu, and stomach upsets."

3. *Enhanced self-esteem:* when as individuals, we begin to mark out time to do what we enjoy. You "send a positive message to your subconscious, and this can go a long way toward discouraging negative self-talk and your critical inner voice." Self-care helps you to be in tune with yourself; it gives a sense of self-worth. When you can meet your needs in the midst of being entangled in the web of other people's needs, it does feel good.

4. *Increased self-knowledge:* incorporating self-care into your routine requires exploring many options. You will need to figure out what will work for you and how it will fit your schedule and budget. Katherine Hurst describes this as "an exercise that helps you think about what you really love to do." The practice of figuring out what makes you feel passionate and inspired can help you understand yourself a lot better.

5. *More to give:* we can only fill other people's buckets if our own bucket is full. It will be difficult to fill from an empty bucket. According to her, "Self-care rejuvenates, and you can bounce back and be supportive to those around you."

When we think about self-care, we are quick to think about money and "wasting" the precious time we do not have much of, rather than understanding and embracing the benefits derived from it. We will always be busy; we are active builders. As mentioned earlier, twenty-four hours will never be enough, and our to-do list will always be endless! There is a need to intentionally invest time and money into ourselves as well. Some self-care ideas are what we just allow to fly past us.

Katherine Hurst categorizes self-care into five major groups.

1. *Sensory self-care:* these are calming activities that involve all our five senses (sight, touch, sound, and smell). This usually consists of engaging one or more or all of the senses at once. Some examples highlighted by Kathrine are but not limited to:

   - Cuddling up under a soft blanket
   - Focusing on the movements of your own breathing
   - Feeling the water on your skin during a warm or cold bath
   - Lying down and listening to soft music with your eyes closed
   - Going for a massage and enjoying your time alone

   As builders, we can connect with a few friends who share similar interests. We can be a support for each other in building self-care into our routine. The book of Ecclesiastes 4:9-10a (NIV) summarizes the importance of having support: *"Two are better than one because they have a good reward for their labor: If either of them falls down, one can help the other up."*

2. *Emotional self-care:* Kathrine Hurst advises on the need to be fully engaged with our emotions, and facing those head-on helps reduce stress. Not coming to terms with our feelings is not a healthy habit or lifestyle. We are God's workmanship created unto good works. We are designed to have feelings. No emotional feeling is wrong, but our responses to such emotions are what matters. The Bible says in Ephesians 4:26 (KJV), *"Be angry, and not sin; let not sun go down upon* your *wrath."* This means sorting out our issues and problems before we go to bed and not depriving ourselves of good sleep. No builder will want to appear at

57

the building site visibly upset. No one will be willing to work with an angry co-builder.

Some examples of emotional self-care are: firstly, be totally honest with yourself about your emotions. Try as much as possible to be with friends or family members whose company you enjoy. If there is a need to cry, please feel free to do so. I tell you: you will feel better afterward! Make time to laugh. Amuse yourself. Delve into the archives and dig out memories (pictures are a good one).

3. *Physical self-care:* this involves engaging in physical activities. Examples, as highlighted by Katherine, are but not limited to:
   - Going to the gym or looking up physical exercise techniques you can do in the comfort of your own home online.
   - Go for runs, jogs, or walks—either alone or with a friend.
   - Go cycling
   - Join a class and learn something new—sports, cooking, baking, or a musical instrument.

4. *Social self-care*: this might look different to different people, whether you are an introvert or extrovert. Connecting with people "helps us combat loneliness and isolation." Self-care is about doing "things with people who really make you feel good." Some social self-care ideas are:
   - Have a lunch or dinner date with a friend. Choose a place both of you will enjoy and savor the time and meal together.
   - Practice reaching out to people, especially those not within your immediate sphere of influence.
   - Avoid socializing with those who undermine or disempower you.

- Meet new people.
- Strike up exciting conversations with people but be mindful of personal boundaries.

Self-care is a huge part of parenting. Parenting is the one "job" you cannot resign from. You cannot call in sick, and you are always on duty attending to everyone's physical, mental, and emotional needs. So, listening to your own need should not be seen (even by you) as selfish. We should set out time to take naps and have the required hours of sleep to stay mentally and physically refreshing. Time and commitment are of great importance to self-care rather than the money that we mostly think of.

You can prayerfully consider what self-care activities will work for you and fit into your overall family schedule. Then work hard at it and stay committed.

At any point that we feel overwhelmed, it is vital to seek support. Asking for help should not be seen as a sign of weakness but rather as a sign of strength. Below are some ideas of activities we can carry out with our children and the whole family.

- Cook or bake together.
- Work on homework.
- Play sports together.
- Attend a concert, show, or movie together.
- Shopping trip.
- Have a family movie or game night.
- Go on a bike ride or walk together.
- Read a book together—this works great for younger children.
- Make a craft or start a project together.
- Make yourself available for your child to teach you something; this can be empowering for the child.
- Or just simply ask the child what they would like to do!

The list is endless. The last chapter in this book provides you with the opportunity to list fun activities you can do together with your children or as a family. At some point, you might create individual time for each child but still make time to come together as a family and have fun.

What if things did not go as planned? We should remember that when building, after setting everything in place, there are situations that things might not work—like electrical or plumbing faults, for example. That does not mean we did not put in our very best or did our due diligence.

Investment of Money

The investment of money and time can complement each other. Both tools can bring out the best in each other.

Which is more important, money or time?

If you can, you can have this as a group discussion. This is not meant to declare a winner, but rather to stir up thought-provoking, healthy conversations. It can make us more aware of what we are investing in and how we invest in our children.

At times, I have been caught up in the web of wanting to provide all the things I missed as a child for my children. Then I had to challenge my motive, and I realized I was meeting my needs and not theirs. I had to be truthful with myself.

We might have all the time in the world, but we would also need to make some financial commitments. We should be ready and willing to spend money. Most of the items might not appear affordable, but it is worth the investment! There are many resources to help our children on their spiritual journey so that, as they grow in age, they are growing spiritually. We should be intentional about this.

Below is a list of resources (but not limited to)

- Bibles
- Books
- CDs and DVDs
- Bible trivia and Bible quizzes

- Puzzles
- Coloring and activity books
- Board games
- Bibliopoly (Bible-based Monopoly)
- Crafts items

The list is endless …

The items highlighted above help us bond with our children and develop good relationships. Some of the activities, depending on the child's age, will help develop excellent motor skills. This is the ability to use their smaller muscles, like pinching and threading. This will translate to life skill activities such as lacing their shoes, buttoning their jackets, turning doorknobs, etc. As the children can practice these life skills themselves, they get better at them, and life becomes easier for us all. By His grace!

Exercise

My top five self-care practices I want to commit to are:

_____

_____

_____

_____

Challenges to the above are

_____

_____

_____

_____

(Do find time to evaluate your commitment to the above list).

Money, time, or both. Which is more important to invest in your children, and why?

_____

_____

_____

_____

Tool #4

Building Talents

Seest thou a man diligent in his business? he shall stand before kings; he shall not stand before mean men."
Proverbs 22:29 (KJV)

"Your talent is God's gift to you. What you do with it is your gift back to God."
Leo Buscaglia

What is Talent?

Talent is "the natural ability someone has to do something well without being taught" (Cambridge Dictionary).[21]

In Matthew 25:14–30, Jesus gives an account of the Parable of the Talents where the master gives talent to "every man according to his ability." The talent can be referred to as money, skills, or an ability that one has been given, but in this scripture, it is referred to as a unit of monetary value.

In verse 15, the master did not give everyone equal amounts of talent: he gave it "according to his ability." Is the master unfair? Was he showing favoritism? Why did everyone not receive equal amounts of talents? Will not the number of talents have a direct impact on the outcome?

It is so easy for us to look at others and think we would perform better if only we had the same opportunities in life. Everyone has what they need to succeed in life "according to our abilities." All they need to do is develop it.

According to Ray Hollenbach, in his article for the Billy Graham ministry, he called our attention to the difference between stewards and owners. He also asked, "Do we see ourselves as stewards or owners?"[22] In his explanation of the difference, he said, "A steward lives for the day he will return the master's goods to Him. An owner believes his possessions are his to spend in any way he sees fit. All we have: our material goods, abilities, and even our very lives belong to someone else. We are merely holding them for the day of reckoning." The master will hold every one of us accountable for what He has committed into our hands. This includes all the children He has blessed us; biological, spiritual, and those He has placed in our sphere of influence. The Master will undoubtedly return, and we will have to give account!

The first and the second servant put their talents to use, and they were multiplied. The master commended them for their faithfulness "in little" and made them rulers over much. The third steward buried his talent and was later given to the individual who was faithful with his. Our perception of the value we place on what we have (our talents) might affect our choices in life. The servant with the one talent might have viewed what was given to him as nothing compared to what the other servants had. This might have impacted his decision to have "digged in the earth and hid his lord's money." Our revelational knowledge of Christ as the God who knows and sees all will help us understand and accept that He gives everyone, "according to our own ability."

Hugh Whelchel, in his Five Lessons for Our Lives from the Parable of the Talents, highlights that the parable teaches that success is a product of our work. We are to put our talent to good use. We are to invest our time and money and "use our talents to glorify God, serve the common good, and further God's kingdom, and use all the talents God has given us to produce the return expected by The Master,"[23]

The parable also teaches us that God always gives us everything we need to do what he has called us to do. The individual who got one talent got as much as every other person if he had put it to good use. He has given us, "according to our ability." He said God expects us to generate a return by using our talents toward productive ends. The servants were given enough to produce more. The servants with five and two talents did, but the servant with one talent did not!

The parable further teaches us we are not all created the same. Everyone upon the surface of the earth is unique in skills and abilities. The master gave each servant, "according to his ability." According to Whelchel, "The master understood that the one-talent servant was not capable of producing as much as the five-talent servant." The giver knows the ability and capability of each servant. Giving the one-talent servant five talents might amount to setting him up for failure. But all servants will require effort to reproduce.

We should also understand that each child is unique but not created empty. Children from the same family might possess different talents and skillsets. As parents, we should encourage our children to appreciate whatever talent they have and help them develop it! The Bible declares in 2 Corinthians 10:12 (KJV)," but *they are measuring themselves by themselves, and comparing themselves are not wise.*"

The parable teaches us that we work for the master and not our own selfish purposes. The talent given to these servants does not belong to them; they were only stewards commissioned to put the talent to good use (invest). The Bible says in Psalms 127:3 (NLT) that *"children are a gift from the Lord; they are a reward from Him."* Whelchel encourages us to "maximize the use of our talents not for our own selfish purposes but to honor God." We should feel the satisfaction and joy from doing our best with what God has given us.

Finally, the parable teaches us that we will be held accountable. There is a need to live a life of accountability. These servants knew their master would be back and would inquire of them what they had done with the talents. The one-talent servant did not waste the talent given to him. He did not squander it or throw it away, but "he wasted an opportunity," according to Whelchel. We are responsible for what we do for God with what we have been given, and one day, we will be held accountable. Let us live each day as if by the end of the day, we will need to give account.

The Importance of Talents

Discovering your child's talent helps you to appreciate both the giver of the child and the talent given. With knowledge of your child's ability, you have a tool to work with to influence the life of the child to serve God and humanity.

It gives a sense of purpose and direction to the one who has discovered it.

It is imperative to recognize your unique gifts or talents, traits, or creative strengths to live a life of purpose. It is important to note that the talent is not just for us to keep like the one-talent servant but to invest it like the two and five-talent servants. Our talent should be used as our instrument of service to God and to the benefit of mankind.

Investment and Value of Talents.

The meaning and importance of talents should be explained to children early in life. The skill, sport, or activity they are good at, and enjoy doing effortlessly, is a talent, and it is from God. The talent is to worship God, serve humanity, and better the owner's life. Understanding the importance of what you have helps shape the value you place on it.

Assure the child of your support by building a nurturing environment in which the talent will be developed, and the child can thrive. The support should not be limited to when everything is going well, but also in low moments. Let them know we are there to support them. Remember, the thief cometh to steal, kill, and destroy (see John 10:10). He also comes, *"as a roaring lion, walketh about, seeking whom he may devour."* He will not see the talents God has deposited in their lives to destroy, in Jesus' mighty name! (see 1 Peter 5:8).

Prayerfully Discover Your Children's Talents

Joyce Meyers, in her book *The Power of Being Thankful*, says that prayer should be "the first option, not the last resort." It is not too early to start praying for the child upon conception. The prayer is not for the child to have a talent or that God should please give the child a talent. In reference to our Bible text, each servant was given talents, just not the same measure. As parents, we should pray that God will open our spiritual eyes to identify the talent each child has. Even after discovering the talents or talent the child has, we might be quick to begin to compare with other children. Let us not be quick to compare children (see 2 Corinthians 10:12). Let us be wise builders and not fall into the category of those the Bible refers to as not wise. Even physical houses differ in structure and contents. Children are unique in their ways; no two children are the same. Even identical twins are not identical in every way.

Twins are two babies who are a product of the same pregnancy. They can be identical or fraternal twins. Identical twins are when one fertilized egg (zygote) splits into two to form two embryos. Fraternal twins, on the other hand, are formed from two individually fertilized eggs. Joseph Bennington-Castro, in his write-up "The Mystery of How Identical Twins Develop Different Personalities,"[24] stated that the individuality that emerges from identical twins "has remained a bit of a mystery." To science, it is a mystery, but to our God, who gives accordingly, there is no mystery! He also pointed out how the environment influences the way our genes are expressed. Children born into the same household might operate under different environments. Each child is unique in their choices, tastes, individual experiences, interpretation of their world, and adaptability to their environment. So, even identical twins might share so many similarities, but there are differences in some areas.

God has given each one of them according to their ability. As parents and caregivers, we should be mindful, respect, and celebrate the individuality of each child. Parenting is not one size fits all. God has given these children talents according to their abilities. The first child might be the one with one talent, the second might be the one with two talents, and the last child might be the one with five talents! They should be identified and celebrated individually. These talents might complement each other, or a talent in one child can trigger talents in another child. A nurturing, learning, warm, non-toxic environment should be created to help the child enjoy and develop their talent.

The Bible has the account of Jacob and Esau in Genesis 25:19-34. For the purpose of this book, we will focus on the individual talents each child possesses, though they were twins.

In this account (see Genesis 25: 19 – 34), Jacob and Esau were born to Isaac and Rebekah. The Bible did not state if they were identical or not. Still, the Bible described Esau as *"hairy and a skillful hunter,"* while Jacob was described as a *"quiet man, staying among tents"* (verse 25). Esau in the modern day can be described as an extrovert, and Jacob an introvert. From the Bible description of these two individuals, their physical features, characteristics, skills, and talents were as different as the two children. Did Rachel and Isaac encourage and celebrate the uniqueness of each child? Each parent identified the talents in their children but chose to have favorites rather than celebrate, build, invest, and encourage each child's talent.

The Bible recorded in Genesis 25:28 (KJV), *"And Isaac loved Esau because he did eat of his venison: but Rebekah loved Jacob."* Two unique individual talents that the parents did not harness but instead sidelined for their own use. I can imagine Jacob at home helping with dishes and laundry, always available to run errands, and making quick dashes to the stores for mom. (I would love a son like that!) Esau, on the other hand, was on the field, being "the man," not sitting at home with women chit-chatting away (every man's dream for a son!). Each parent has chosen based on their own expectation of how a child should be.

I cannot stress it enough: every child is unique and given talent according to their own ability, by their maker, the giver of good gifts. That skill that the child carries out effortlessly and enjoys should be encouraged, supported, and built. As parents, we should foster opportunities and positive learning environments for children to diligently develop their talents.

Exercise

Let us look inwards.

My talents are.........

_____

_____

_____

_____

_____

The talents I notice/ have noticed in my child/ren are....

_____

_____

_____

_____

_____

Practical ways I can support my child/ren develop their talents are...

_____

_____

_____

_____

_____

My perceived challenges are……….. *(examples: money, time, work, I do not drive, etc.)*

_____

_____

_____

_____

_____

Tool #5
Building the Builder

Consistency is key! According to Dictionary.com, consistency is "constantly adhering to the same principles, course or form."[25] Children prefer a predictable world; there is a need for parents and caregivers to be consistent in their approach to parenting. A builder must be consistent in the tools, methods, and materials used in the project for best results and minimal frustrations. There will be times of setbacks, disappointments, frustrations, anxiety, etc. Still, we are committed to seeing the project through. Commitment is merely saying, "I will push ahead, irrespective of frustrating external factors!"

Building a strong spiritual foundation for our children, putting effort, investing resources, and taking time to take care of ourselves can be overwhelming. According to Michael Grose, in "How Consistency Improves Kids' Behavior,"[26] "one of the simplest ways to improve a child's behavior is to be more consistent." He also stated that "children love their parents to be consistent as they can predict how they will act. A consistent approach to discipline helps put kids in control of their behavior."

There is a school of thought that believes parents should be unpredictable, keeping children on their toes, where parents can catch them unawares. Consistency, according to Michael Grose, means as parents, "we follow through and do as we say we will. It means resisting giving kids second and third and many chances when they do not comply with rules. Both parents in a dual-parent family get to make decisions together and respond in similar ways." Amos 3:3 (KJV) asks, *"Can two walk together, except they be agreed?"* The New Living Translation of the Bible passage says, *"Can two people walk together without agreeing on the direction?"*

All parties involved in a child's life should always agree on what to do. Consider building an actual house, where the plumber is not in agreement with the electrician. It can cause dysfunction, and the house may not be built correctly. Michael also warned against children playing parents against each other when their standards differ, or communication is poor. So, parents need to be consistent with how they react when children behave poorly or when they do not abide by standards set. All should be on the same page.

Understanding Expectations

Parents should be aware of the burden of expectations on their children. Expectations should be commensurate to the child's age and level of development. Expectations should not be vague but communicated in simple and straightforward language. Children should know what is expected of them, and the consequences should they not follow through with agreed-upon instructions. At times, as parents and caregivers, our expectations of our children are imbedded in societal expectations of us bringing up perfect children. We should understand that these children have expectations of themselves as well. This can be stressful!

According to Michael Grose, "Children like limits,"[27] and they also like to push boundaries. He mentioned in his write-up about a study that has shown that kids will push parental boundaries about one-third of the time. He also stated, "Some toddlers and teens will push twice that amount, which is very hard work indeed." He also explains that "when parents are tired, stretched, and overworked, the last thing we want to do is engage in a battle with a strong-willed child over what are sometimes petty issues. Besides, consistency can make a well-meaning parent who values relationships feel downright awful."

Giving in, rather than being assertive, is not a smart long-term strategy. When you give in quickly and often, after a while, the children will learn you cannot hold on for too long. This might hurt any strategy you want to put in place. It will not take long for them to know the parent that can easily be won over. Consistency is about being strong! It takes some backbone to be consistent. Any parent that feels they would need support in this area can seek assistance from families, friends, or professionals.

Below are some ideas, as highlighted by Michael Grose, to help us be consistent with our children.

- Focus on priority. It is challenging to be consistent with every single behavior a child presents. There is a need to be mindful and focus on one or two areas at a time. Also, the area of focus is not limited to the child. As a parent or caregiver, you might want to focus on areas of development for yourself, such as what can I do for self-care? How can I invest in my child's talent?

- Give yourself a tangible reminder about the changes you are making. You can leave a note somewhere or keep a notebook or calendar telling yourself what you need to do and when to do it. For example, when you need to read to your child, have gadget-free family time, etc.

- Check your routines. Michael advises us to have simple routines. When we have complicated clustered routines, frustration is likely to set in. So, let us keep our routines simple!

- Act rather than over talk. As Michael puts it, "It is inconvenient to set a consequence, as you may have to battle a tantrum that follows. But the stand-firm approach pays off in the long-term as kids learn eventually that you mean what you say and say what you mean." He refers to this as a "firm, consistent discipline." This might not be easy. I speak as a parent. I have learned to practice being consistent and assertive. I certainly agree with Michael that it pays off in the long run. How long is the "long run?" Or how long should it be? That is all relative. We are dealing with young individuals who will want to express themselves but not necessarily with words. Exercising, practicing, and exhibiting the fruit of the spirit, as stated in Galatians 5:22-23 (KJV). *"But the fruit of the spirit is love, joy, peace, longsuffering, gentleness, goodness, faith, meekness, temperance; against all, there is no law."* They come in handy during these periods.

A housebuilder must be experienced and knowledgeable in knowing the right tools and materials to engage and at what stage. As parents and caregivers, we need to invest in ourselves as well. In building a strong spiritual foundation for our children, we should strive to be strong builders. We also need to come up with creative ways of building up ourselves spiritually. One idea I have prayerfully come up with to build myself (by His grace, not by my power) is to pray on the go. I have come to terms with the fact that having a time set aside to pray at home at times does not work for me. So, I pray as I drive to work or, if the weather permits, I go for a prayer walk during my lunch hour. Also, I realized I was not spending as much dedicated time with the word of God. The way I remedied this was to head straight to work after dropping my daughter off in the morning and find a corner to study a few chapters of the Bible before the beginning of the business day. This has worked for me to the glory of God. There have also been times I stayed at home instead of rushing out in the morning to pray or study a chapter or two. This is not cast in stone for me. I have had to tweak it a little bit, but I know I can only build if I am strong! That strength I get from staying in His presence!

Before we explore Cindy McMenamin's "10 Ways to Grow Spiritually: Breaking the complacency habit," let us first explore complacency and contentment and what sets them apart from each other.

Complacency vs. Contentment

According to the Cambridge Dictionary,[28] complacency is "a feeling of calm and satisfaction with your own abilities or situations that prevents you from trying harder," while contentment, on the other hand, is "a state of happiness and satisfaction."[29] Satisfaction comes from not having everything you want but being okay with whom you are and what you have. The Bible states in I Timothy 6:6 (KJV), *"But Godliness with contentment is great gain"'* (KJV). That you have Jesus to meet and supply all your needs is assuring enough.

The difference between complacency and contentment is a delicate one but put merely, contentment is a feeling of satisfaction with what you have, where you are, or who you are. You do not feel stuck; you strive to move forward. Complacency, on the other hand, is being satisfied with what you have, where you are, and who you are, and refusing to work to improve or push yourself out of your comfort zone. As a builder, ask yourself: Am I a complacent or a contented builder?

10 Ways to Grow Spiritually by Cindi McMenamin[30]

1. ***Read through the Bible in a year.*** Her advice is to team up with a friend, agree on a plan, and hold each other accountable. There are several useful resources available to help you do this. If you have already done it, do it again, maybe in a different translation. In your reading, try to pick up memory verses. The verses can be what you meditate on throughout the day, and by the end of the year, you would have memorized hundreds of verses.

2. ***Choose a Bible study plan.*** At this point, we go beyond just reading the Bible or just checking off a to-do list. According to the Cambridge Dictionary, reading is "the skill or activity of getting information from books or an occasion when something is written, especially a work of literature."[31] On the other hand, studying is "the application of the mind to the acquisition of knowledge, as by reading, investigation or reflection, which requires long hours of study."

3. ***Choosing to study the Bible transcends merely reading the Bible.*** As Cindy puts it, "go beneath the surface, uncover the truths, principles, and insights in Scripture." The agreed plan or personal plan might be a character study, study by books, or alphabetical order. Whatever method you might want to choose, just go beyond reading. The Bible tells us in Joshua 1:8 (KJV), *"This book of the law shall not depart out of thy mouth; but thou shalt meditate therein day and night, that thou mayest observe to do according to all that is written therein: for then thou shalt make thy way prosperous, and then thou shalt have good success."*

4. ***Study a topic that will help you grow.*** Cindy advises us to set goals and be aware of the areas we want to grow. Also, at this point, I might want to ask myself: Am I content with my spiritual state and my walk with the Lord, or am I just complacent? My genuine answer to this question will determine my level of thirst to know God more and want to grow spiritually. In her example, Cindy stated, "if you want to know Him more, consider a study of His names in the Old Testament and Jesus' 'I am' statements in the New Testament." If you need to slow down and learn to listen for His voice, study all the Word says about rest or hearing His voice. If these are character traits that you know you need to work on, consider an in-depth study of some or all the fruits of the spirit as mentioned earlier" (see Galatians 5:22- 23).

5. ***Participate in a small weekly group Bible study.*** Lead one among your friends, neighbors, or co-workers. We can grow at a faster rate in the community because we can share our experiences with one another and hold each other accountable. The Lord also tells us about the need for fellowship in Hebrews 20:25 (KJV). *"Not forsaking the assembling of ourselves*

together, as the manner of some is but exhorting one another: and so much the more, as ye see the day approaching."

6. ***Read books to deepen your devotional life***. Investing in our spiritual growth should not be limited to studying the Bible. We should also spend our time and money on books and other Christian literature. Cindy advises to "set a goal to read a book every month, every three months, or whatever is realistic for you." Reading one book per month has not worked for me, but like she advised, "whatever is realistic for you." Let your goals be **SMART.**

    a. ***Simple:*** State your goal (s) in simple words or terms, e.g., studying three chapters pcr day.

    b. ***Measurable***: Have the means to evaluate yourself. Check how you are doing every Monday.

    c. ***Attainable***: Let it be what you can handle, considering all other activities you might he involved in. Sincc I want to keep growing in the knowledge of the word of God, setting a goal of finishing (studying) the Old Testament in one month is unattainable for me: at least right now. Set a goal that genuinely works for you without being complacent.

    d. ***Relevant***: How does that goal contribute to attaining your overall spiritual growth?

    e. ***Time-bound***: There should be a time frame attached to the goal. When do I want to finish this book? One week? Two days? It should not be an ongoing project.

The Bible states in Habakkuk 2:2 (KJV), *"And the Lord answered me and said, 'Write the vision and make it plain upon tables, that he may run that readeth it.'"* There is a need to write down our goals clearly and simply. Goals are better worked on when written down and not when they are in our heads. I always say to those around me: How will my life be without sticky notes?! I just love to have that visual reminder. Also, in setting goals for our children as we build, let those goals be SMART.

7. **Start a weekly prayer group.** You can start one or join one with others who share similar concerns on your heart. Cindy gave some examples like "praying with other moms for your children. Praying with other wives for unsaved spouses. Praying during your lunch hour with co-workers or praying with friends or church members for a specific burden God has placed on your heart."

8. **Start a journal to record your growth.** Journaling might be a habit most of us are not used to, or we see it as a waste of time. At times, the burden of carrying one around might be what we would not like to deal with. I can say it is worth it! She mentioned she had contacted people who have shared with her how journaling has helped them. Cindy puts it like this: "As you read the Word, how did a certain passage compel you to pray? What changes are you asking God to make in your life? What discoveries have you made about His character or His word? Write it down and date each page. By the end of the year, you'll have a record of where God took you and what He has shown you through the past 12 months."

9. **Record your blessings and answered prayers.** Keep a "blessing book," according to Cindy, in which you record every blessing that comes your way throughout the year, adding a prayer of thanks or praise. Moreover, write out your prayer requests and register the answers as they come. This will help us to have a heart of gratitude and become one who does *"everything without murmurings and disputing"* (Philippians 2:14 KJV). Furthermore, be a person who *"in everything gives thanks: for this is the will of God in Christ Jesus"* (1 Thessalonians 5:18 KJV). Personally, I write out my prayer points at the beginning

of the year. As I study and pray through the year, once there is a physical manifestation of answered prayers, I put the date beside the prayer point. Also, as I study, I jot down my lessons, prayer points, and action points. These have helped me significantly in my walk with the Lord.

10. ***Disciple a young believer***. "We learn the most when we teach it to others. And seeing them grasp truth for the first time gives it a fresh impact on our lives as well," Cindy stated, and I cannot agree more. I have had the opportunity to share that; there are times when your needs are met as you try to help other people meet their needs. This has been my story. When you are teaching someone or mentoring someone, you are equally getting better.

Prayerfully choose what works for you, commit to it, and as you go and grow, you can add to it. You might only be able to commit to studying the Bible and memorizing Bible verses. You might not be comfortable to disciple anyone yet or read more than one book in a month. Whatever stage you are, are you content or complacent? Cindy also stated in her write-up that "spiritual complacency isn't ever an intention, but too often it can creep into our lives unnoticed—a tragic consequence of failing to be intentional in our spiritual growth."

One thing I know about growth is that it is desirable and worth the investment of our time and money. Growth in everything good and Godly: it is what we all should intentionally strive for.

Our growth should also be measurable. What is the yardstick I am using to measure the level of my spiritual growth? I try to measure as the Lord adds another year to my life, so as I grow in age, I grow in my walk with the Lord. Most often, we are mindful of our physical body weight; some people like me check our body weight every day. How many of us check our spiritual weight daily? How did I fare today? Did I tell someone about the love of Christ today? Did I pray for or with someone today? Did I go out of my way to meet the needs of someone today? These and many more are ways (I feel) we can daily check our spiritual weight.

We learn as we grow, and we grow as we learn. There is no spiritual height that I can attain that I think will be satisfactory. I join apostle Paul to declare, *"No, dear brothers and sisters, I have not achieved it, but I focus on this one thing: forgetting the past and looking forward to what lies ahead"* (Philippians 3:13 NLT).

There are so many areas in which I am still trusting God for growth. I forget the past failures, hold unto the lessons learned from them. I focus on attaining my goal, which is building a solid spiritual foundation for my children so that when the wind, fire, and flood of life rage, they can stand by His grace!

Exercise

Let us explore consistency vs. complacency

In what areas have I been consistent regarding parenting?

_____

_____

_____

_____

_____

In what areas have I been complacent regarding parenting?

_____

_____

_____

_____

Thoughts

_____

_____

_____

_____

_____

Tool #6:

Recommendations for Parents

Children don't come with a manual. They are also not to be fixed. Every family is unique, so is every child in the family. I have, by the grace of God, four beautiful children with four different personalities. What has worked for me at various stages of my life might not work for you. One thing I have learned—the hard way—is that children are quick to learn what they see you do faster than what you sit them down to teach them. I do not know the gravity of my influence on my children until I see them display a certain behavior that I have noticed myself expressed in the past. I saw my youngest daughter pointing her finger while talking to someone. I considered this rude. Then I found myself displaying the same behavior while I was trying to correct her. At that point, I became more aware and mindful of my actions.

Since we want our children to grow, become independent, and be responsible members of society, we need to work on ourselves first. We need to look inward and deal with those attributes we do not want our children to inherit from us. We need to work at becoming good and Godly role models for our children.

A role model is "an individual who is looked up to and revered by someone else. A role model is someone other people aspire to be like, either in the present or in the future" (Business Dictionary)[32]. Human beings are imitators by nature; we see people, fashion trends, and quickly copy them. This can either be good or bad.

Being a Godly role model not only to our children but also to everyone within our sphere of influence is a blessing. Children need parents and caregivers to demonstrate what it means to be a genuine follower of Christ and a lover of God. In choosing a role model, the yardstick is essential: What are their core values? What is his or her salvation story? What we learn from our role models will eventually be what will be transferred to the person who has chosen us as a role model. The individual you select should be one who has based their life on the word of God and demonstrates that.

Below are some Bible verses that talk about being Godly role models and seeing Christ as our own perfect example and role model.

Continue to live such upright lives among the
gentiles that, when they slander you as practices of
evil, they may see your good actions and glorify
God when he visits them.
(1 Peter 2:12 ISV)

Let no one look down on your youthfulness, but
rather in speech, conduct, love, faith, and purity,
show yourself an example of those who believe.
(1 Timothy 4:12 NASB)

Remember your leaders who taught you the word
of God. Think of all the good that has come from
their lives and follow the example of their faith.
(Hebrews 13:7 NLT)

And you should imitate me, just as I imitate
Christ.
(1 Corinthians 11:1 NLT)

*For God called you to do good, even if it means
suffering, just as Christ suffered for you. He is your
example, and you must follow in his steps.*
(1 Peter 2:21 NLT)

*He that saith he abideth in him ought himself also
so to walk, even as he walked.*
(1 John 2:6 KJV)

*I have given you an example to follow. Do as I
have done to you.*
(John 13:15 NLT)

Being a Godly Role Model Parent

*Fathers, do not exasperate your children; instead,
bring them up in the training and instruction of the
Lord.*
(Ephesians 6:4 NIV)

*Train up a child in the way he should go: and when
he is old, he will not depart from it.*
(Proverbs 22:6 KJV)

*But take heed lest by any means this liberty of
yours become a stumbling block to them that are
weak. For if any man sees thee which hast
knowledge sit at meat in the idol's temple, shall not
the conscience of him which is weak be
emboldened to eat those things which are offered to
idols.*
(1 Corinthians 8:9-10 KJV)

When you sin against them in this way and wound their weak conscience, you sin against Christ.
(1 Corinthians 8:12 NIV)

A good reputation is more desirable than great wealth and favorable acceptance more than silver and gold.
(Proverbs 22:1 NET)

Abstain from every form of evil.
(1 Thessalonians 5:22 NLT)

But the fruit of the Spirit is love, joy, peace, forbearance, kindness, goodness, faithfulness, gentleness, and self-control. Against such things there is no law.
(Galatians 5:22-23 NIV)

Join together in following my example, brothers and sisters, and just as you have us as a model, keep your eyes on those who live as we do.
(Philippians 3:17 NIV)

Because our gospel came to you not simply with words but also with power, with the Holy Spirit and deep conviction. You know how we lived among you for your sake. You became imitators of us and of the Lord, for you welcomed the message in the midst of severe suffering with the joy given by the Holy Spirit. And so, you became a model to all the believers in Macedonia and Achaia.
(1 Thessalonians 1:5-7 NIV)

*For you, yourselves know how you ought to follow
our example. We were not idle when we were with
you, nor did we eat anyone's food without paying
for it. On the contrary, we worked night and day,
laboring and toiling so that we would not be a
burden to any of you. We did this, not because we
do not have the right to such help, but in order to
offer ourselves as a model for you to imitate.*
(2 Thessalonians 3:7-9 NIV)

Being a role model to others is very important. The Bible declares that we are to be "the light of the world," and that we are "set on a hill," so we ought not to be hidden (See Matthew 5:14). The function of light is to shine and light the path for others. God can use our light to draw men unto Himself, not by what we say to them only, but what they see us do.

As parents and caregivers, we should be proud of our children when they replicate our actions. We should not only be role models to our children but everyone we come into contact with.

I ask myself this question, "how much influence do I have over my child?" You might ask yourself as well, and then explore your emotions in light of God's word.

Pastor Don Jones of the West Glendale Baptist Church said, "Unfortunately, many of our young people look to athletes and popular musicians to find their examples."[33] He stated this is not specific to any nation or country, that "this crisis exists in our country, politics to be specific, our homes, and yes, even our churches."

I am convinced that we need more leaders that actively demonstrate how to live life with integrity and character. In other words, what you say and do in your daily living should have a lasting and positive impact on someone else. In 2 Timothy 1:5, apostle Paul has this to say about the young man, Timothy. *"When I call to remembrance the unfeigned faith that is in thee, which dwelt first in thy grandmother Lois, and thy mother Eunice; and I am persuaded that in thee also."* From this Scripture, we can deduce that Timothy's mother and grandmother were Godly role models. Timothy's faith can be attributed to the Godly influence his mother and grandmother had on him.

To be a role model who represents God well in all we do, we should let the word of God dwell in us richly. We should hide it in our hearts that we might not engage in foolish and ungodly activities.

Are Role Models Important?

I remember when I was growing up, there were some aunties I admired and wanted to be like. As young as I was, the qualities I liked ranged from how they dressed, spoke, and even walked! At that point, it had nothing to do with intellect, but just what my young eyes could see. For others, it might be a parent, an aunt, a cousin, or an uncle. Like my situation then, it was intentional. Still, in some other cases, it might be unintentional, and we might not know how these individuals are influencing us.

As I grew (and I am still growing and learning) in age, maturity, academics, and career, my role models changed. We might just appreciate and want to emulate some specific characteristics we have seen, so we pray to God to have those same characteristics manifest in our lives. It is not enough just to have any role model. We need to seek out good and Godly ones. That is of high importance. Our actions and outlook in life are influenced by the individual we look up to. We are to strive to be like them in all we do (so long as they are also imitating Christ) and even to surpass their godly achievements. Even our Lord Jesus told us we will do more than He did when He was on the earth (See John 14:12). According to Gwen Steller, role models "are meant to be examples, not templates." We are not to copy all they do in totality; role models have their flaws as well. We need to be sensitive and choose to consider God's word and leading.

Below are some traits of a godly role model
- God-fearing
- Honest about their successes and failures
- Self-motivated

- Ever-learning and striving to get better as well
- A resilient individual
- Does what he or she preaches

As parents and caregivers, let us seek to be role models for our children. Our children can know about our successes and failures, the ups and downs we have gone through. This will not paint us as bad parents, but rather, they will learn from us. I would not want my children to go through life without having someone who will have a positive influence on them or who they are accountable to. It might be dangerous not having a role model.

Role models are not gender specific. A male child can have someone of the opposite sex as a role model. When your child has a different gender as a role model, the role model is older. We could explore the traits and attributes that made your child choose the individual as a role model in the first place. We can ask some open-ended questions and, where appropriate, support their decision or raise concerns where necessary and not an outright condemnation of their choices or actions.

Seek Out Information

A builder of a physical structure will seek out the right materials for the project and know how to put these materials to beneficial use. He will be mindful of what to seek (information, materials, and manpower), where to find them (the source), and how to put them to good use (wisdom, experience).

Below are some Bible passages about the importance of seeking knowledge.

The heart of the prudent getteth knowledge, and the ear of the wise seeketh knowledge.
(Proverbs 18:15 KJV)

The heart of Him that hath understanding seeketh knowledge: but the mouth of fools feedeth on foolishness.
(Proverbs 15:14 KJV)

I love them that love me; and those that seek me early shall find me.
(Proverbs 8:17 KJV)

Then ye shall call upon me, and ye shall go up and pray unto me, and I will harken unto you. And ye shall seek me and find me when ye shall search for me with all your heart.
(Jeremiah 29:12 -13 KJV)

But seek ye first the kingdom of God and his righteousness and all these things shall be added unto you.
(Matthew 6:33 KJV)

    Seeking, according to the English translation online dictionary, is "to try to get something, especially something that is not a physical object," "to attempt to find something," or to "attempt or desire to obtain or achieve something."[34] One thing that is common to all definitions is the effort to try something. As Hugh Whelchel puts it, "'You don't know what you don't know."[35] Whelchel stresses the importance of putting the information gathered to good use. It is possible to have all the information about resources but still be skeptical about using them.

    Do we know where to get what information from? The Bible (the building plan) is the only true template of life. It can never be outdated. At whatever stage of building (the child), we can always consult it. No matter the part of the world you are in, seek to know the resources around you. Although some parts of the world have more resources than others, we live in a global village, where we can travel the world in the palm of our hands. Videos on how to set up parental controls can be found on the Internet. It is full of research studies on children's and teen's mental health, habits, and lifestyles and their impact on their physical, psychological, and emotional development.

The local news is also a good source of getting to know what is going on in our immediate environment and communities. We can be a significant contributor and policy influencer in our community by being an active member of the community through volunteering.

According to Lexico, a volunteer is a "person who freely offers to take part in an enterprise or undertake a task"[36] or an individual who "freely offers to do something."[37] It is also someone who "does something, especially helping other people willingly and without being forced or paid" (Cambridge Dictionary).[38] Even in situations or societies where there are no structured volunteering programs, we can still find a way around it once we have a willing heart.

From the above definition, a volunteer does not get paid, but being a volunteer is a worthy investment of our time. At times, it can be challenging when you are trying to settle in a new country as a newly landed immigrant. You are being encouraged to volunteer when bills are gradually pilling up (from personal experience). You just feel that precious time can be spent making money. Volunteering is not just a place to help others; it is a way to better ourselves. Your child's school and your immediate community are a good starting point. Most schools often send out emails stating volunteering opportunities for parents. Let us find time for these activities as often as we can. Volunteering is not a lifetime commitment. As we explore the importance of volunteering below, I will use my experience as a case study.

Some importance of volunteering

- *Learn new skills*
- *Focus less on yourself*
- *Connections*
- *Fun*
- *Giving back*

By volunteering, you can meet with other co-builders who are in your child's life. These include schoolteachers, sports coaches, Sunday school teachers, other parents, etc. With constant and consistent interactions with co-builders, you know their value systems and beliefs.

As a significant builder, decide if you want them to be part of your child's life or use that as teaching moments to emphasize and reiterate your value system and belief.

You can volunteer in your child's school, either in the classroom or at events. The volunteer hours can be tailored to suit your availability. Your immediate or local community is also an excellent place to invest your time and energy. Your immediate community refers to your immediate environment, like your street, while your local community transcends your immediate environment. There are various advertised volunteer positions, ranging from board members, event planners, social media persons, board secretary, etc. As we have discussed in chapter five, you know your talents, so explore those areas and thrive. You can also volunteer in a particular sector and learn new skills.

Role Model by Volunteering

By volunteering, we can be good role models. Not just to our children, but also to everyone in our sphere of influence, letting them know the importance and benefits of volunteering.

What the Bible says about Volunteering

Dear children, let us not love with words or speech but with actions and in truth.
(1 John 3: 18 NIV)

Each of you should use whatever gift you have received to serve others, as faithful stewards of God's grace in its various forms.
(1 Peter 4:10 NIV)

In everything I did, I showed you that by this kind of hard work we must help the weak, remembering the words the Lord Jesus himself said: 'It is more blessed to give than to receive.'
(Acts 20:35 NIV)

For we are God's handiwork, created in Christ Jesus to do good works, which God prepared in advance for us to do.
(Ephesians 2:10 NIV)

Carry each other's burdens, and in this way you will fulfill the law of Christ.
(Galatians 6:2 NIV)

If you extend your soul to the hungry and satisfy the afflicted soul, then your light shall dawn in the darkness, and your darkness shall be as the noonday.
(Isaiah 58:10 NKJV)

For I was hungry and you gave me something to eat, I was thirsty and you gave me something to drink, I was a stranger and you invited me in.
(Matthew 25:35 NIV)

Keep on loving one another as brothers and sisters. [2]Do not forget to show hospitality to strangers, for by so doing some people have shown hospitality to angels without knowing it. [3]Continue to remember those in prison as if you were together with them in prison, and those who are mistreated as if you yourselves were suffering.
(Hebrews 13: 1 -3 NIV)

For even the Son of Man did not come to be served, but to serve, and to give his life as a ransom for many.
(Mark 10:45 NIV)

Exercise

Let us explore

What are the traits you desire to see in a role model?

_____

_____

_____

_____

_____

Who was your role model when you were growing up? What were the traits you saw in them?

_____

_____

_____

_____

_____

Will you choose a role model for your child/ren?
Give your answer with reason.

_____

_____

_____

_____

_____

Have you ever volunteered before now? YES or NO
(Please circle your answer)

If NO, give two reasons why.

_____

_____

_____

_____

_____

If YES, state two benefits to you as an individual.

_____

_____

_____

_____

_____

What NEW volunteering opportunities would you like to explore?

_____

_____

_____

_____

What are the steps you would like to take towards volunteering,
if you have never volunteered before?

_____

_____

_____

_____

_____

What are the volunteering opportunities you want to explore for your child/ren?

_____

_____

_____

_____

_____

Tool #7

The Final Tool

Prayer is the key!

Philippians 4:6 *"Do not be anxious about or worried about anything, but in everything (every circumstance and situation) by prayer and petition with thanksgiving, continue to make your (specific) request known to God"* Amplified Bible (AMP).

Although this chapter is about prayers for our children, we also need to pray for ourselves first as parents and builders. You cannot fill an empty cup from an empty bucket. Here is my personal testimony. A couple of years ago, I was praying, and on top of the list was to pray for my son, who was very young and active. As I lifted my voice to pray, I heard the voice of the Lord said to me, "Pray for yourself." It came as a shock to me; I cried my eyes out! The revelation I got was that I would need grace for what I was about to face. So, I prayed for myself for grace, wisdom, and direction. We were living in Holland then.

In the same way, I want us to approach praying for our children using the word of God. Let us pray for ourselves first and everyone involved in our children or child's lives at every point.

Suggested prayers for parents and caregivers

They were all trying to frighten us, thinking, "Their hands will get too weak for the work, and it will not be completed." But I prayed, "Now strengthen my hands."
(Nehemiah 6:9 NIV)

Prayer
Lord, strengthen my hand to build. Lord, strengthen my physical, spiritual, emotional, and financial hand to build, in Jesus' mighty name. Amen!

Situations will arise that will make you question your authority in Christ Jesus or put your parenting skills and ability to test. All these are to weaken and distract you. Stay focused, refuse to be distracted, and refuse to give up on any child. The blood of Jesus was shared for them too.

If any of you lack wisdom, let him ask of God, that giveth to all men liberally, and upbraideth not; and it shall be given him.
(James 1:5 KJV)

In all that we do, we need wisdom, which is the application of knowledge. As builders, there is a need to apply wisdom when putting all the resources together. We need to know when and how to use each tool we are engaging at every point.

Prayer
Lord, grant unto me wisdom to be a wise builder and grace to build wisely, in Jesus mighty name. Amen!

I will instruct thee and teach thee in the way which thou shalt go. I will guide thee with mine eye.
(Psalms 32:8 KJV)

It can be soothing to know that as we (builders) build (children), we have a manual (Bible). We have one who is wiser and better than us, giving us instructions, teaching us, and watching over us.

Prayer

Lord, grant me divine direction as I build these lives, show me the way to go. Lord, do not allow me to fall, fail, or operate in error. In Jesus mighty name. Amen!

Suggested prayers for children

I am challenged like never before by Debbie McDaniel. In her article "40 Powerful Blessings to Pray Over Your Children,"[39] she wrote, "Children are a gift - an amazing blessing from God. Every single day we may find ourselves doing a lot for our kids, loving, and caring for them, nurturing, training, helping, equipping, encouraging, protecting, and doing so much more." I can attest to it that, as caring caregivers, and parents, this is all part of our daily routine, no matter the age, development, or gender of the child or children.

She also wrote, "We spend money on sports, lessons, and various classes to help them grow and become all they can be, providing opportunities for them to do what they most love in this world." She asked, "Are we praying God's powerful word and promises over their lives?" I have also continually asked myself this question, and I am prompted to pray even more for God's heritage under my care.

Debbie advises, "We should never underestimate the importance of speaking blessings and truth over their lives." It is not enough to have strategies in place; prayer is the master key that can unlock the potentials in our lives and that of our children.

Shall we pray...

The salvation of their soul:

Acts 16:32 (ESV) says, *"Believe in the Lord Jesus, and you will be saved, you and your household."* John 3:16 (NIV) says, *"For God so loved the world that he gave his one and only Son, that whoever believes in him shall not perish but have eternal life."*

Prayer
Lord, we pray for the genuine salvation of the souls of our children and grace to continue to live for you. In Jesus' mighty name, Amen!

The indwelling of the Spirit of God
Isaiah 11:2 KJV says, *"And the spirit of the LORD shall rest upon him, the spirit of wisdom and understanding, the spirit of counsel and might, the spirit of knowledge and of the fear of the LORD."*

Prayer
Lord, we pray that the spirit of God will guide and guard our children and that they will live in fear of You all the days of their lives. In Jesus' mighty name. Amen!

Submission
"Submit yourselves therefore to God. Resist the devil, and he will flee from you." James 4:7 KJV.

Prayer
Lord, we pray that You will give our children the grace to live a life of submission to Your will and grace to resist every form of temptation. In Jesus' mighty name. Amen!

Godly Relationships
"Whoever walks with the wise becomes wise, but the companion of fools will suffer harm." Proverbs 13:20 ESV.

Prayer
Let us pray that God will surround our children with Godly mentors and role models. In Jesus' mighty name. Amen!

Courage

"Be strong and courageous. Do not be afraid; do not be discouraged, for the Lord your God will be with you wherever you go." Joshua 1:9 NIV. *"For the Spirit God gave us does not make us timid, but gives us power, love and self-discipline."* 2 Timothy 1:7 NIV.

Prayer
Let us pray that our children will not be timid, and that they will be bold to stand for what is good and Godly. In Jesus' mighty name. Amen!

Contentment

"Don't love money; be satisfied with what you have. For God has said, "I will never fail you. I will never abandon you." Hebrews 13:5 NLT.

Prayer
Lord, give our children the grace to live a life of contentment and to trust in you as their provider. In Jesus' mighty name. Amen!

Integrity

"Whoever walks in integrity walks securely, but he who makes his ways crooked will be found out" Proverbs 10:9 NIV.

Prayer
Let us pray that God will make them responsible and honest children, growing up to be people of integrity. In Jesus' mighty name. Amen!

Wise Instruction

"All your children will be taught by the LORD, and great will be their peace." Isaiah 54:13 NIV.

Prayer

Let us pray that the God of Heaven Himself will teach our children, they will not be troubled children, and they will enjoy the peace of God all the days of their lives. In Jesus' mighty name. Amen!

Safety

"*The LORD will guard your going out and your coming in from this time forth and forever.*" Psalms 121:8 NASB.

Prayer

Let us pray that our children will be safe from every form of calamity. In Jesus' mighty name. Amen!

Obedience

"*Children, obey your parents in the Lord, for this is right.*" Ephesians 6:1 NIV.

Prayer

Let us pray that our children will not be rebellious. They will be respectful and dutiful, in Jesus' mighty name. Amen!

Personal Prayer Points for your child/ren

_____

_____

_____

_____

_____

_____

_____

_____

_____

_____

_____

_____

_____

_____

_____

Conclusion

The uniqueness of every family is characterized by their socio-economic status, number, and ages of children, physical environment, and their value system. No two families are the same. A tool that works for my family might not work for yours

The Bible declares in 2 Corinthians 9:10 (NIV), *" 'Now he who supplies seed to the sower and bread for food will also supply and increase your store of seed and will enlarge the harvest of your righteousness."* God is the giver of children; He has given us these "seeds" to invest our time, energy, and resources. He will also supply everything that is needed to bring up. The Bible says in Matthew 7:7-8 (KJV), *" 'Ask, and it shall be given you, seek and ye shall find; knock, and it shall be opened unto you: For every one that asketh receiveth; and he that seeketh findeth and to him that knocketh it shall be opened."*

The door of heaven is available for each of us to knock on whenever we need guidance and direction. I have been at some crossroads in my life regarding parenting and felt discouraged, frustrated, and helpless. At this point, prayers were not what was on my mind, because I was too tired and weak to pray. But at such times, I know the only option for me is prayers! Let us learn to ask the Father of all wisdom, as His words encourage us in James 1:5 (NLT). *"If anyone lacks wisdom, you should ask God, who gives generously to all without finding fault, and it will be given to you."*

Let us also learn to *"Pour out your heart like water in the presence of the Lord. Lift up your hands to him for the lives of your children…"* (Lamentations 2:19 KJV).

107

Conclusion

To him, who believes, all things are possible; trust God that as you pray and declare God's word over your children, it shall come to pass. Their lives will be a manifestation of answered prayers! (see Mark 9:24).

As was mentioned in chapter four, we can develop the habit of writing down our prayer points, and as they are answered, we can put a check against them and date it. We should also not be discouraged; if things are not turning out the way we imagined. Isaiah 55:8 (NLT) says, *"For my thoughts are nothing like your thoughts says the Lord, and my ways are far beyond anything you can imagine."* The answer might not unfold the way we have envisaged it. God is the God of the total picture. He can see the end from the beginning. He is a God of love who has our best interest at heart. All we need to do is to trust Him, engage the tools, and build!!!

Lest we forget….
- Prayer is the foundational tool
- The Bible is our manual
- Every child is unique
- Children do not come with a manual
- Parenting is not a one size fit all
- Volunteering is beneficial to all
- Technology is not a way out
- Dare to know
- Selfcare is not selfish
- The 3-6-9-12 rule

Happy Building!!!

References

Page 15
1 Meredith Olson, January 19, 2018. What is the meaning of Train up a child in a way he should go. Accessed April 2, 2019 - https://bit.ly/2PdOK38

Page 25
2 Fisher Centre for Alzheimer's Research Foundation
Janelle Cox Teaching Strategies for Vocabulary Expansion TeachHUB.com.
Accessed May 2, 2019
(www.teachhub.com/teaching-strategies-vocabulary-expansion.html)
(www.businessdictionary.com/definition/creative-thinking.html)
Lin, Y. (2011) Fostering creativity through education – a conceptual framework of creative pedagogy. Creative Education 2 (3) 149–155.

Page 28
3 Kimberly Young June 29, 2017, Children and Technology: Parents Guidelines for Every Age Technology and Society Accessed May 20, 2019 - https://bit.ly/30erybk

Page 29
4 What Richard Branson and Suze Orman Know About Having (and Being) the Ideal Mentor - tinyurl.com/y86wfvu6-

Page 29
5 Wikipedia definition for mentorship -
https://en.wikipedia.org/wiki/Mentorship

Page 34
6 Goodreads Benjamin Franklin Quotable Quote - shorturl.at/uCHUY

Page 35
7 Day2Day Parenting October 21, 2013, Normal attention Span By Age
https://day2dayparenting.com/

Page 36
8 Katherine Lee Last Updated January 21, 2019, Kids on Screentime: What research says about the impact on Health and Development Verywell Family Accessed April 14, 2019 - www.verywellfamily.com

Page 36
9 The Lancet Child and Adolescent Health Journal - https://www.thelancet.com/journals/lanchi/home

Page 36
10 Wikipedia dictionary definition for Longitudinal study - https://en.wikipedia.org/wiki/Longitudinal_study

Page 37
11 Children and Technology: Parent Guidelines for Every Age - https://bit.ly/2DoCvOF

Page 39
12 Meriam Webster dictionary definition for malnutrition - https://www.merriam-webster.com/dictionary/malnutrition

Page 40
13 Elana Pearly Ben-Joseph Reviewed April 2018 Internet Safety KidsHealth Accessed May 20, 2019 - https://kidshealth.org/en/parents/net-safety.html

Page 43
14 The Concerns About Kids and Screen Time - https://bit.ly/3jYXzfo

Page 45
15 Cheryl, M 2019 'Parenting the Video Fanatic: How to encourage other interest,' Calgary Child Magazine, Jan. /Feb., p.66, 69

Page 45
16 Cheryl, M 2019 'Parenting the Video Fanatic: How to encourage other interest,' Calgary Child Magazine, Jan. /Feb., p.66, 69

Page 47
17 Learners Dictionary definition for recreation
https://www.learnersdictionary.com/definition/recreation

Page 52
18 Cambridge dictionary definition for diligent -
https://dictionary.cambridge.org/dictionary/english/diligent. Accessed
January 7, 2019

Page 52
19 Meriam Webster dictionary definition for time - https://www.meriam-
webster.com/dictionary/time. Accessed January 7, 2019

Page 55
20 Katherine Hurst What is Self-Care, and why is Self-care Important? The
Law of Attraction.com Accessed December 2018
(http://www.thelawofattraction.com/self-care-tips/)

Page 63
21 Meriam Webster dictionary definition for time - https://www.meriam-
webster.com/dictionary/talent

Page 64
22 Ray Hollenbach March 16, 2019, The Parable of the Talents Billy Graham
Evangelistic Association Accessed January 20, 2019
(https://billygraham.org/story/the-parable-of-the-talents/)

Page 64
23 Hugh Whelchel   March 14, 2013, Five Lessons for our lives from the
Parable of the Talents the Institute of Faith Works and Economics Accessed
January 2019 (https://tifwe.org/talents)

Page 67
24 Joseph Bennington- Castro May 09, 2013, The Mystery of How Identical
Twins Develop Different Personalities Genetic Literacy Project-
shorturl.at/eimuV

Page 73
25 Dictionary definition for consistency -
https://www.dictionary.com/browse/consistency?s=t

Page 73
26 Micheal Grose - The Incredible Years
http://www.incredibleyears.com/parents-teachers/articles-for-parents/

Page 74
27 Micheal Grose - The Incredible Years
http://www.incredibleyears.com/parents-teachers/articles-for-parents/

Page 77
28 Cambridge dictionary definition for complacency -
https://dictionary.cambridge.org/us/dictionary/english/complacency

Page 77
29 Lexico dictionary definition for contentment -
https://www.lexico.com/en/definition/contentment

Page 77
30 Cindy McMenamin December 2011 Complacency Habit: 10 Ways to Grow
Spiritually: Breaking the complacency Habit. Accessed May 2019
https://tinyurl.com/y9hfwc56

Page 78
31 Cambridge dictionary definition of reading -
https://tinyurl.com/ybxdgngh

Page 85
32 Business dictionary definition of role models -
http://www.businessdictionary.com/definition/role-model.html

Page 89
33 Pastor Don Jones of June 19, 2006, Role Models West Glendale Baptist
Church https://www.sermoncentral.com/sermons/role-models-don-jones-
sermon-on-christian-disciplines-92283?ref=SermonSerps Accessed
November 20, 2108

Page 92
34 https://www.meriam-webster.com/dictionary/seeking
Accessed May 2019

Page 92
35 You Don't Know What You Don't Know: Knowledge, Understanding, and Wisdom - https://tinyurl.com/y9bslj26

Page 93
36 Lexico dictionary definition of volunteer -
https://www.lexico.com/definition/volunteer

Page 93
37 English terms dictionary definition for volunteer -
https://terms_en.enacademic.com/45893/volunteer

Page 93
38 Cambridge dictionary definition for volunteer -
https://dictionary.cambridge.org/us/dictionary/english/volunteer

Page 101
39 Debbie McDaniel 40 Powerful prayers to pray over our children
(https://www.crosswalk.com). Accessed July 2019.
 https://www.crosswalk.com/faith/prayer/40-powerful-blessings-to-pray-over-your-children.html

BUILT FOR **ETERNITY**

With

IRETE FAMILY

(Daniel, Patience, Angel, Esther, Anita and Alex)